D0069874

LAWMEN

Volume 14

True Tales of the Old West

by

Charles L. Convis

DISCARDED

PIONEER PRESS, CARSON CITY, NEVADA

LIBRARY
CALDWELL COMMUNITY COLLEGE
HUDSON, NC

Copyright © 2000 by Charles L. Convis
All Rights Reserved
Manufactured in the United States of America

Library of Congress Catalog Card Number: 96-68502

03-04 BTM. 90

ISBN 1-892156-04-0 (Volume)
ISBN 0-9651954-0-6 (Series)

03-04

Printed by
KNI, Incorporated
Anaheim, California

CONTENTS

ILLUSTRATIONS

MISSOURI MYSTERY

Justice was swift in Jackson County, Missouri, in 1864. When a jury found Jebb Sharp and Dick Merrick guilty of murder in the killing of John Bascum, the judge sentenced them to hang at next dawn.

Deputy Sheriff Cliff Stewart, the county executioner, always selected a few of the rougher set, who didn't mind the work, to do the job under his supervision. For dawn hangings he first treated his helpers to a breakfast on the county, served with an abundance of whiskey. On this occasion the revelers tarried longer than usual, and dawn was upon them before they knew it. Stewart picked two of the soberest guests and sent them for Sharp and Merrick.

"How'll we know which ones to bring?" they asked.

"Two upstairs at the far end. There's only four, and they got their names over the doors. You can't hardly miss."

The rest of the party rode to the Missouri River bottom, where three hundred persons had gathered to watch the spectacle. Stewart joined friends on the bank.

The two men, blindfolded and gagged, were brought to the hanging tree. Ropes were quickly placed and the pair launched into eternity.

A special crew buried the men. Stewart did not stay; he hurried back to fill out the papers showing that the court order had been followed.

As he was writing, he heard a familiar voice holler down for a cup of coffee before his hanging. Stewart hurried upstairs, sick to his stomach. Sharp was holding out a tin cup between the bars of the cell where he and Merrick waited.

At first Stewart thought his helpers got the wrong pair. But when he looked, the other pair were also in their cell. Stewart rushed downstairs, cursing his helpers for grabbing the first pair of men they found in the jail. But every prisoner was in his proper cell, not a single man missing!

Stewart ran outside, jumped on his horse, and galloped back toward the river bottom. He met a group which included the pair who had brought the men to be hanged.

"Who did you hang, you idiots?" Stewart demanded. "Sharp and Merrick are still in jail. Where'd you get the two you brought?"

"Right where you told us."

"You're lying. Those men are still in jail."

"Look here, Stewart, we been helping you a long time.

We never make no mistake. We got them just where you said, and don't go calling us liars."

"Come back and see for yourself."

They galloped back to the jail and Stewart showed them that Sharp and Merrick were still in their cell.

"Did anybody come up this morning to take you fellows out?" Stewart asked Sharp.

"Not a soul. We was expecting someone, but nobody showed up."

The two men responsible for the mistake insisted that they had taken the two men out of the cell which had Sharp's and Merrick's names on it. They pointed to the men in the other cell. "Just ask them. They musta saw us."

"All right," Stewart said, turning to the other two cellmates. "Were these fellows up here this morning?"

"If they was, we didn't see them."

A sheriff's investigation showed that two drunks had been brought in and left by the arresting officer to be booked. The night jailer insisted that the two had walked out while he was in the toilet. Cells on the second tier stood open and empty, but none had been used.

The men hanged by mistake were dug up, but neither could be identified. The night jailer and the arresting officer both swore that they were not the drunks that had been brought in for booking.

A six-weeks investigation produced no answers. Some claimed that friends of the condemned men had keys to the jail and made the switch. But how could they assume that Stewart, who knew both Sharp and Merrick, would not see that the wrong men had been brought to the hanging tree? And if Sharp and Merrick had friends who could do that, why were the two men still in the jail after the mistake was discovered? If they had left, no one would have known of the mistake.

Stewart and the night jailer both lost their jobs. Sharp and Merrick were sent to prison by the judge. He said that since they had not been hanged on the prescribed date, he could not order them hanged again. Later he ordered them released, saying that since the jury had prescribed the death penalty, they could not be imprisoned. No one knows to this day who was hanged in their place.

Suggested reading: Tom Bailey, "Mystery at the End of a Hangman's Rope" in *Frontier Times, Fall, 1958.)*

DEAD SHOT

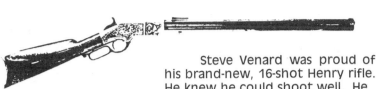

Steve Venard was proud of his brand-new, 16-shot Henry rifle. He knew he could shoot well. He also learned, when the chips were down, that his courage matched his marksmanship.

Even though Venard had once been a marshal in the California foothills, Grass Valley and Nevada City citizens didn't know the strength of his heart and nerves until May 15, 1866. Early that morning, three masked men held up the Wells Fargo stage on its way from North San Juan to Nevada City.

"They had a bunch of tools on the ground where they stopped us," one passenger said. "Looked like a regular blacksmith shop."

"Yeah," said Cal Olmstead, the driver. "They blew the express box wide open. "Had around eight to nine thousand dollars in it."

"They took my pistol," another passenger said. "Unloaded it and handed it back, just as cool as could be."

"You see where they went?" asked Sheriff R. B. Gentry.

"They're on foot," Olmstead answered. "Headed up into those rocky ravines above the stage road. They're so full of loose boulders and chaparral, a man can't hardly walk in them. Be hell to follow their trail."

"Yeah, a needle in a haystack. Well armed, were they?"

"They each had two pistols that I could see."

"I'll need five men so we'll have three pairs to hunt for their trail," Gentry said, loking at Venard. "Steve, will you come?"

"Surely will. I'll get my new Henry."

Gentry soon had four more men. The posse reached the holdup scene before noon.

Venard and James Lee paired together and started up a steep, dry gulch covered with head-high chaparral and thick brush. Loose boulders shifted under their feet as they moved carefully, their eyes keen.

They traveled a half mile searching for scrapes on rocks and broken twigs. Finally, Venard spoke.

"I'm satisfied we got the right track, Jim. You head back to get the others."

"You better wait here, Steve. Keep going up alone, they'll be looking right down your throat."

"I won't be far."

When Lee left, Venard continued up the gulch. He moved stealthily, listening for any sound, watching for the slightest movement. Now and then a rock would slide under his feet, and he would freeze, his body tense, his heart pounding, his eyes boring into the brush ahead.

After he had gone another half-mile, Venard heard the click of a pistol being cocked. He whirled, threw the Henry to his shoulder and fired. One of the robbers fell, not over fifteen feet away.

"I didn't dare move," he told the citizens later. "If I'd turned around to look for a hiding place, they would have got me in the back. I couldn't go forward, as we were practically on top of each other already. I just stood still, watching and listening."

Then he heard another click behind a large rock. He waited until a pistol muzzle moved upward. He fired again, before the man behind the rock could get a shot off.

The third man ran and Venard fired at him.

The sheriff and the rest of the posse heard the three shots. They came running, were relieved to see Venard still on his feet.

"Reckon I got all three," he said, but I didn't want to look close until you got here to help."

The first robber had been shot through the heart, the second through the forehead, and the third close enough to the heart to die instantly.

"You didn't waste any bullets, Steve," Gentry said.

"Didn't need to. This new rifle shoots pretty good."

About forty citizens gathered in the afternoon and tried to climb to the scene of the shooting. A dozen were unable to do it. One of the climbers loosened a large boulder which bounded down, flying completely over the three dead robbers, as they lay on flat ground waiting transportation to the inquest.

All the money was recovered. Wells Fargo decided to pay Venard a $3000 reward after the dead robbers were brought in. His Henry rifle is now in the Wells Fargo Museum in San Francisco.

One of the robbers, Jack Williams, had been operating in the area for months. The others, Bob Flynn and George Moore, had each escaped twice from San Quentin. The three came to their end in one of the West's most memorable moments in law enforcement.

Suggested reading: *Grass Valley Union*, May 16, 17, 1866.

MAN HUNTER

Bass Reeves was born a slave in Lamar County, Texas, in 1838. He got into a fight with his owner, knocked him unconscious, and ran away to Indian Territory.

Reeves fought with Indians on the Union side in the Civil War. When the Union Indians retreated north to Kansas, Bass stayed behind to join Union guerrillas and Indian home guards.

After the war, bandits, horse thieves, and train robbers flocked to the territory. Reeves found work as a guide and interpreter for the U. S. marshals. In 1875 two hundred more deputy marshals were hired to stay ahead of the outlaws. Reeves was proud to get one of the new stars.

Bass Reeves was six feet two inches of rock-hard muscle. He could whip any two men in a bare-fisted fight.

Reeves enjoyed detective work. He used many aliases and often posed as a farmer, outlaw, or tramp to find his man. He became the most feared and best man hunter in Indian Territory.

Once, Reeves learned that four outlaws were hiding in an abandoned cabin in Pottawatomie County. He borrowed a yoke of old oxen and a broken down wagon. Dressed as a poor tenant farmer, he drove toward the cabin. He got the wagon stuck on a stump and waited for the outlaws to come to his aid. When the four men had pushed the wagon free, Reeves drew his pistols and disarmed them. He chained them together and padlocked the chain to the wagon. He loaded the wagon with the thieves' loot and marched his prisoners thirty miles to the county seat.

One of Reeves' most famous gunfights was in June, 1884, when he fought Jim Webb, the foreman of the large Washington Ranch in the Chickasaw Nation. The year before, a black preacher on a small ranch next to the Washington Ranch had started a grass fire. The fire got out of control and reached Webb's ranch. After a violent argument about the fire, Webb had killed the preacher.

Reeves got the warrant for Webb's arrest. After a short gunfight with one of Webb's men, Reeves took Webb into custody. Webb posted bail and failed to appear for his trial.

A new warrant was sent to Reeves to bring Webb in. He learned that Webb was hiding near the Arbuckle Mountains, deep in the Chickasaw Nation. As Reeves rode up to a store in what is now Woodford, Oklahoma, Webb jumped though a window and ran for his horse.

Reeves shouted to Webb to surrender. He rode forward, cutting Webb off from his horse. Webb ran into the underbrush with Reeves still demanding his surrender. When Webb realized he could not escape, he whirled around and began firing his rifle. His first shot hit Reeves' saddle horn, the second cut a button from his coat, and the third tore the reins out of his hand.

Reeves jumped from his horse, jerking his rifle from its scabbard. As Reeves landed on his feet, Webb's fourth shot hit his hat. Reeves fired twice from five hundred yards. A hand could have covered both wounds in Webb's chest. He dropped to the ground, dead.

Reeves's closest call also came in 1884. He was riding the Seminole Whiskey Trail with warrants for four men, when three other men ambushed him and forced him to dismount at gun point. Recognizing that he had warrants for those men also, he asked them what day it was so he could put it down on their arrest records. The men, holding Reeves in their gun sights, laughed uproariously. Reeves drew, shot two of the men dead before they could fire, and then grabbed the third man's gun from his hand as he was firing it. He crashed that weapon down on the head of its owner, killing him.

Reeves said he killed fourteen men, all in the line of duty, in making over three thousand arrests. Some question the line of duty part on one killing. Reeves, himself, was tried in 1887 for murdering his cook.

One version was that Reeves and the cook got into an argument by their campfire. The argument became heated in more ways than one when the cook threw boiling grease on Reeves' pet dog. Reeves, furious, shot the cook, who fell into the fire. Reeves was so mad he let the cook lie there awhile before pulling the body out.

At trial, Reeves denied that version. He said the argument was trivial and the shooting accidental. He was found not guilty.

Bass Reeves never learned to read or write. He memorized his orders from verbal instructions. In his many gunfights he was never wounded. He died of natural causes in 1910.

Suggested reading: Art T. Burton, "Bass Reeves, Deputy U.S. Marshal," in *True West* (Dec. 1991).

MYSTERIOUS DAVE

Dave Mather, born in Connecticut in 1845, was a descendant of Cotton Mather, the Salem witch hunter. A slender, stoop shouldered man with dark brooding eyes and a gunfighter's drooping mustache, his quiet moodiness led to his nickname, Mysterious Dave. He first showed up in the West as a cattle rustler in Arkansas in 1873.

The next year he had moved to Dodge City, taking up gambling and hunting buffalo. An unhappy loser in one of his card games shoved a knife between Dave's ribs, nearly killing him. Dodge City's first major surgery saved his life, and he got a part-time appointment as a peace officer. This began his career as an itinerant — sometime officer, sometime outlaw.

Like many others of that time, Dave was equally comfortable on either side of the law. He spent about as much time in town jails as he did wearing their badges.

For a time Mather and Wyatt Earp sold gold painted bricks in Mobeetie, Texas. They told the cowboys the bricks came from a mine hidden by priests during the Spanish conquest, and they needed money to finance an expedition to recover the rest of the treasure. But the sheriff bought a brick, found out it was phony, and ordered them out of town. They split up, Mather going to Las Vegas, New Mexico, one of the toughest towns in the West. There he became a deputy city marshal.

In January, 1880, Mather got his first test as a lawman. He and Marshal Joe Carson charged into a saloon and opened fire on a four-man gang who refused to check their guns with the bartender. The gang, all under twenty-one, filled Carson with bullets, killing him instantly. But Mather, not wounded, killed one of the gang and wounded two others, Tom Henry and James West. John Dorsey, the fourth gang member was not hit. Henry and Dorsey escaped.

Three weeks later the two fugitives were captured and lodged in jail with James West, still alive from the shootout. That night Mather, forgetting that he wore a star, led a mob on the jail. They dragged the prisoners to a makeshift gallows.

West, unable to stand, was the first one hanged. He struggled with the rope and screamed for his mother.

At that moment Marshal Carson's widow opened fire on Henry and Dorsey. Henry, painfully wounded, crawled to the edge of the scaffold platform and begged someone to shoot him in the head. Within seconds the two men and the hanging body of West were filled with bullets. The coroner reported that the men met their just fate at the hands of parties unknown.

Mather moved on to Dodge City. He left there in April for Colorado, accompanied by ex-sheriff and ex-marshal Charles Basset. Then Mather returned to Texas. He lived for a time with Georgia Morgan, a black madam in Dallas. When he left without notice, she discovered that her jewelry was missing.

When the *Las Vegas Gazette* heard the Texas news, they remembered Mather's escapades while a marshal in their town, and they gleefully reported: "We trust he'll soon be dancing a mid-air jig."

Mather returned to Dodge City to become assistant marshal in town and deputy sheriff in Ford County. When Bill Tilghman became marshal he replaced Mather with Tom Nixon, but Mather kept the deputy sheriff job. Then he and Nixon got into a feud, perhaps because Mather had a secret relationship with Nixon's wife.

On July 18, 1884, Nixon and Mather tangled on the inside stairs of the opera house. Nixon's bullet left Mather with splinters in a finger and powder burns on the face. Nixon ran outside, bragging that he had killed Mather.

Three days later, Mather emptied his pistol into Nixon. "I shoulda killed him six months ago," Mather said. The jury acquitted him of murder, saying Nixon had it coming. Bat Masterson was one of the defense witnesses. One of Mather's bullets had also killed a sleeping dog. The jury ruled that shooting also justified, as any dog should have known better than to go to sleep in a Dodge City saloon.

In May, 1885, Mather and his brother, Josiah, were involved in a saloon gunfight in Dodge City in which David Barnes was killed. Dave Mather and Barnes had been playing cards before the fight broke out. Mather was shot in the head, but his gun was not fired during the fight, so it appears that Josiah killed Barnes. Neither brother was brought to trial.

Later in 1885 Dave Mather was appointed city marshal of New Kiowa, Kansas. No one knows for sure what happened to him after that. Some say he went to Canada and became a member of the Northwest Mounted Police. His brother said Dave Mather was killed by moonshiners in the mountains of Tennessee.

But no one knows.

Suggested reading: Leon C. Metz, *The Shooters* (El Paso: Mangan Books, 1976).

JACK OF ALL TRADES; MASTER OF MANY

Seth Bullock, twenty-year-old Canadian, came to Helena, Montana Territory, in 1867. The successful prospector was elected to the territorial senate in 1871. His horseback reconnaissance of the Yellowstone country led to the creation of the nation's first national park.

Bullock became sheriff of Lewis and Clark County in 1873. While in that office, he faced down a lynch mob and later personally hanged the first man legally executed in the territory.

Bullock and business partner Solomon Starr shipped a supply of hardware down the Missouri River and freighted it overland to Deadwood, Dakota Territory. They soon had branch stores in Sturgis, Sundance, Spearfish, and the Carbonate Mining Camp. For some strange reason, one of their early shipments of goods included a large assortment of chamber pots. Bullock auctioned them off in what must have been an entertaining evening of oratory mixed with commercial enterprise. They also carried whiskey, cigars, tea, and condensed milk.

Bullock reached Deadwood on August 1, 1876, the day before Wild Bill Hickok was shot to death in that wild gold camp. No legal process yet existed for the election of public officials, so Bullock became unofficial sheriff by popular demand. When Lawrence County was organized, with Deadwood the county seat, he became the first regularly appointed sheriff.

Bullock soon civilized Deadwood. When disgruntled miners took over the mine which had refused to pay them, Bullock dropped burning sulphur down an air shaft, bringing to a non-lethal end one of the country's first sit-down strikes. He left the sheriff's office in 1878, but continued as a deputy U. S. Marshal.

Bullock had a commanding personality, and his piercing gray eyes could stare down a "mad cobra or a raging rogue elephant." It is reported that he never killed a man in Dakota Territory. "When he went out into the streets under a blazing sun at high noon," his grandson wrote, "he was looking for lunch, not someone to shoot."

Bullock served as president of a mining company and vice president of the Merchants National Bank. He and his partner, Starr, built up a successful ranch on the Belle Fourche River. They brought the country's attention to the value of

SETH BULLOCK
South Dakota State Historical Society

raising irrigated alfalfa for livestock.

In 1884 Bullock rode up to a suspicious-looking group of men whose leader, a deputy U. S. marshal from the northern Dakota Badlands, introduced himself as Theodore Roosevelt. The disheveled band had just captured a horse thief, Crazy Steve, whom Bullock was also trailing. The two deputies liked each other immediately and became life-long friends.

Bullock was captain of Company A of Grigsby's Cowboy Regiment, a Rough-Rider outfit raised for the Spanish-American War. But he could not follow his rough-rider friend, Roosevelt, to Cuba; the regiment sat out the war in a Louisiana training camp.

In 1900 President McKinley, certainly following the advice of vice-president Roosevelt, made Bullock supervisor of the Black Hills National Forest, the first national forest supervisor in the country. In 1905, while walking with Bullock in Washington, President Roosevelt asked him if he would rather be commissioner of the General Land Office or of Indian Affairs. "I need you here with me, Seth," Roosevelt added.

"Mr. President, there's just one job that would get me to live in this town, and you're filling it just fine."

"How about governor of Alaska?"

"I'll stay in the Black Hills."

Roosevelt did appoint him U. S. Marshal, an appointment that continued under Presidents Taft and Wilson.

Roosevelt made many hunting trips to the Black Hills ranch of his friend. His sons learned to ride and hunt and became fine outdoorsmen under Bullock's teaching. Bullock had led a group of fifty cowboys to Washington for Roosevelt's inaugural. They galloped up and down Pennsylvania Avenue, lassoing spectators to the delight of the new president.

When Roosevelt died in 1919, Bullock, then suffering from cancer, led the movement to erect the first monument to his friend in this country. The tall tower, five miles from Deadwood, sits on a mountain now called Mount Roosevelt.

Bullock died in September of that same year. Roosevelt had called him "my ideal American." Bullock wanted just a one-word epitaph on his own tombstone — Pioneer.

Both men had it right.

Suggested reading: Helen Rezatto, *Tales of the Black Hills* (Rapid City: Fenwyn Press, 1989).

SOFT SPOKEN, WITH QUICK FISTS

Abilene's greatest marshal never killed a man. Intelligent and gentle, he neither drank nor gambled, and he never used profanity. He liked children, and he respected women, even the prostitutes.

He had grown up in New York, becoming a professional boxer at fifteen after soundly whipping three waterfront hoodlums who had attacked him. Five years later he joined the police department. But he accidentally killed a 14-year old boy while chasing a thief, and, although held blameless, Tom Smith resigned from the force and headed west.

After army service on the Arizona frontier, Smith became a teamster for the Union Pacific Railroad in its railhead camp at Bear River City, Wyoming. There, his courage and fighting ability got him named law officer for the camp and gave him his popular name, Bear River Tom. In March, 1870, he showed up at Abilene, Kansas, riding a tall gray horse, Silverheels.

"I hear you're looking for a marshal," Bear River Tom said to the mayor.

Were they ever! The citizens of Abilene were fed up with gunplay. Placards announcing a City Council resolution that guns could not be carried in town had been riddled with bullets from rebel-yelling, Texas cowboys. Marshals who lasted a month were old veterans.

The mayor looked Tom over. Thirty years old, the smooth-muscled man moved with athletic grace, but he wore no gun.

"This is no place for a man without a gun."

"If I get the job, let me worry about that."

But the citizens refused to turn a soft-voiced, mild-mannered, unarmed man into an instant corpse, so the mayor said, "no," and sent for two tough cavalrymen from St. Louis.

The troopers reached Abilene one evening and left town the next morning. "We ain't ready to die this quick," they said.

A citizens' committee found Smith back at a railroad construction camp and offered him the job. He took over in June. He soon ran into Steve Roe and Hank Belton, both determined to get rid of the new marshal.

Roe, pistol in hand, faced Smith and sneered, "Marshal, we're your welcoming committee. We're taking you over to the saloon."

"No guns allowed, boys," Smith said softly. "Just hand them over."

Belton roared with laughter, reaching for his gun. "Here's

BEAR RIVER TOM SMITH

Kansas State Historical Society

mine," he shouted, "let's see if you can take it."

Smith's fists moved so fast, no one was sure what had happened, but both men lay unconscious at his feet. He reached down and took their guns. Then other cowboys stepped forward to offer theirs.

"Just leave them with the bartenders," Smith said. "You can pick them up when you leave town."

After one saloon brawl with so many shots fired at Smith that he seemed to have a charmed life, Abilene was quiet for a time. Grateful citizens presented him with a pair of ivory-handed six-guns. He wore them but never drew them.

Smith's quiet control of Abilene ended in November, just five months after he became marshal. Andrew McConnell, a homesteader, had killed his neighbor in a dispute about the neighbor's cattle eating his corn. Smith had warrants for the arrest of McConnell and his partner, Les Miles.

When Smith told McConnell he was under arrest, McConnell shot him twice in the chest. Despite his injuries, Smith wrestled his man to the ground and handcuffed him. But Miles, who had been chopping wood nearby, ran up and clubbed Smith on the head with his gun. Then Miles took his axe and nearly decapitated the brave marshal.

A solemn posse carried the body into Abilene, a town of outraged citizens. The quiet man had brought them law and order with fists that had the speed of striking snakes and the power of hard-swung sledgehammers. Now this rare man had been bushwhacked. McConnell and Miles, soon captured, barely escaping lynching, and both served long prison terms. The town's businesses, including saloons, gambling houses, and brothels closed up for Bear River Tom Smith's funeral. Behind the flower-loaded hearse walked Silverheels, Smith's ivory-handled guns hanging from the empty saddle. Men, women, and children, all wearing crepe and many wiping their eyes, followed the procession down Texas Street, across the railroad, and up to the graveyard.

Later a granite boulder was placed at the grave. It contains a plaque reading:

> Thomas J. Smith died a martyr to duty.
> A fearless hero of frontier days,
> Who in the cowboy chaos,
> Established the supremacy of law.

Suggested reading: Carl W. Breihan, *Great Lawmen of the West* (New York: Bonanza Books, 1963).

SUPER SLEUTH

When a Wells Fargo stage was robbed near Glendale, Oregon, at one a.m. on July 25, 1883, the company sent a dispatch from its San Francisco office to a former Oregon sheriff, asking him to ride down to Glendale and look into the matter. They picked a man they knew through previous service as deputy district attorney, deputy sheriff, and sheriff to be one who could solve crimes.

Over a hundred years ago, crime detection methods were crude compared to today. But the imagination, intelligence, and patience of this man was remarkable. In about twelve hours after the request, and thirty hours after the holdup, Francis Pierce Hogan had the crime solved and the robber arrested.

Hogan, born in Ireland in April, 1848, was in Wisconsin by his first birthday. His parents had emigrated to escape the potato famine. Sixteen-year-old Francis, the oldest of twelve, and his father both enlisted in the Wisconsin infantry near the end of the Civil War.

Francis Hogan homesteaded in Minnesota and studied law in St. Paul. He moved to Roseburg, Oregon, in 1873, just ten years before his remarkable example of detective work.

Hogan spent that ten years as a newspaper editor and in law enforcement, leading to his retirement as sheriff in 1883. But he agreed to continue on a case by case basis with Wells Fargo. He was operating his own general store when he got the dispatch that afternoon of July 25.

That evening Hogan reached Glendale by train and visited the crime scene. He learned that the robber, a six foot, 175 pound man, had been wearing blue overalls. Hogan picked up a glass liquor flask which had an unusual air bubble in it. He returned to Glendale and started asking questions of bartenders.

One bartender remembered selling the flask, filled with whiskey, to a red-haired, bearded man the previous evening. Hogan's inquiries shifted to hotels. A rancher overheard his description and volunteered that he had sold a bay horse and saddle to such a man for sixty dollars that morning. The man had ridden north toward Cow Creek Canyon. Hogan took the train north and learned from some hunters that they had seen such a rider earlier that afternoon.

Hogan borrowed a horse and continued riding north. Just as the sun was rising on July 26 he reached the cabin of Watson Mynatt. Mynatt, working in his field, said a red-headed man riding a bay horse had stopped for the night and was still asleep in his cabin.

Hogan checked the barn. The bay horse was there, with a saddle that fit the rancher's description. As Hogan walked toward the cabin, the door opened and a red-headed man with a beard came out. He wore blue overalls, the pockets sagging heavily. Hogan knew that gold coins totalling $1810 had been taken, including one coin discolored by acid.

"Good morning," the man said, as he laid his revolver down and started washing his hands.

Hogan drew his revolver. "Put up your hands. You stole that horse in the barn from me."

"I did not. I bought it yesterday in Glendale for sixty dollars."

"Let's see how much money you got in your pockets."

It totalled $1750 in gold coins, one of them discolored, exactly sixty dollars less than the amount stolen. Hogan arrested the man. He turned out to be Jim Todd, a robber who had left Montana earlier that year, just ahead of vigilantes.

Todd was convicted of robbery. Before the year was out he was serving life at hard labor in the Oregon state prison. In an interesting aftermath, Hogan was visiting the prison later when Todd recognized him. He reached through the bars of his cell and struck Hogan with a heavy ink bottle, nearly killing him.

Hogan left Roseburg in 1887 for Spokane, where he became a millionaire land developer. He served three times as a delegate to the Democratic national convention. He died in 1927, surviving his wife by two years.

When Hogan told Wells Fargo in 1887 that he would no longer be able to accept assignments regarding stage holdups, the chief detective for the company wrote, thanking him for fourteen years of help.

"Your success in ferreting out and bringing to justice so many notorious outlaws and on numerous occasions recovering the stolen treasures was a valued contribution, not only to the firm but to law enforcement as well. We regard you as one of the renowned peace officers of the West."

Suggested reading: Gary and Gloria Meier, *Knights of the Whip* (Bellevue; Timeline Publishing Co., 1987).

LAW COMES TO COLORADO CITY

He descended from England's great epic poet, and he grew up in a mansion where his father was governor of Florida, but Jeff Milton became known as a good man with a gun.

Jeff left for Texas at sixteen. Two years later, lying about his age, he joined the Texas Rangers. In 1881, still a year too young to be a ranger, Jeff was camped with his company at Hackberry Springs, near Colorado City, a wild, west Texas town of cowboys and railroad construction crews.

During the organization of Mitchell County, with Colorado City its seat, Ranger Dick Ware had run for sheriff, defeating W. P. Patterson, a local cattleman. Patterson, a poor loser, was arrested by rangers for disturbing the peace. With no jail, the rangers had chained him to a mesquite tree, a humiliating experience for the hot-headed Patterson.

On May 16 Patterson rode into town, spoiling for a fight. Jeff, with rangers Sedberry and Wells, was patrolling the streets just after midnight, when they heard shooting at the Nip and Tuck Saloon. When Patterson and a friend came running out, Sedberry asked who had done the shooting.

"Damned if I know," Patterson said.

"Let's have a look at your pistol," Sedberry said.

"You damned rangers can go straight to hell!"

Sedberry and Wells grabbed Patterson, but he jerked loose and shot at Sedberry, powder-burning him. Jeff dropped Patterson with one shot. Wells, an inexperienced ranger, shot the dying man after he had fallen. The onlookers turned into an angry mob, threatening to hang Milton.

The three rangers gave themselves up to Sheriff Ware, who let them keep their guns and go about their business. Ranger Captain Bryan Marsh galloped in from Hackberry Springs to protect his men from lynching.

The three accused men were fully armed when they reached the courthouse the next day for their examining hearing. Irate cowboys demanded that their guns be taken. With both the rangers and county officials fearing a riot, Jeff agreed that they give up their guns only if they were escorted into the courthouse by rangers and protected by them during the hearing.

So the three accused men and three heavily-armed rangers marched into the courtroom and stood with their backs to the wall. Each armed ranger had two pistols at his belt, one within inches of the accused man standing next to him. There was no trouble.

All three accused were bound over to the grand jury. They returned to the ranger camp. When the grand jury indicted the three, they learned that even though they were being prosecuted for a killing that occurred in the performance of their duty, the state did not provide any funds for their defense. Jeff's relatives hired four lawyers to defend him, including the former attorney general of Texas. It took two years to bring the case to trial.

During the wait, Jeff's company was moved further west to Big Spring. From that camp, Jeff and Buffalo Bill Jenkins were sent to Graham to assist local authorities in enforcing the law. When they learned that the county would not pay for their room and board, Jeff, by then a corporal, took his helper and rode back to the ranger camp. Shortly after, two deputy sheriffs were overpowered by three escaping prisoners. The outlaws and one of the deputies were killed and two townsmen wounded.

"If they had only paid our board," Jeff said, "this would never have happened."

On another assignment Jeff rode across the Rio Grande to capture a fugitive in Mexico. He dropped his rope over the culprit's head and then argued with local officials about returning his prisoner to Texas. When it became obvious that no agreement was to be made, Jeff dallied his rope around his saddle horn and headed for home. The prisoner followed at a fast pace on foot, and no extradition was necessary.

After semi-annual visits to Colorado City to obtain continuances, usually with a ranger escort providing protection from the townspeople, Jeff's case finally came to trial in Abilene in November, 1883.

After the jury retired to deliberate, a prominent cowman approached Jeff. "Son," he said, "if it don't come out right, I want you to know that I got the fastest horse in the county tied out front with a Winchester on the saddle. I can hold them back long enough for you to get a head start."

The help was not needed. All three rangers were acquitted — free again to help bring law and order to the rough frontier in West Texas.

Suggested reading: J. Evetts Haley, *Jeff Milton, a Good Man with a Gun* (Norman: University of Oklahoma Press, 1948).

FREE FROM THE VICES USUALLY FOUND

The grateful citizens of Caldwell, Kansas, presented Henry Newton Brown, 24, a gold-mounted, engraved Winchester rifle in 1882, when he became their marshal. Brown, from nearby Rolla, Missouri, had traveled widely and acquired a reputation as a fearless gunfighter. He was already known as a killer in Texas when he joined Billy the Kid in New Mexico. After many battles as one of the Kid's closest companions, he got a pardon and became a marshal and a deputy sheriff in Texas. He rode up the Chisholm Trail to Caldwell in July 1882, where Marshal Batt Carr, who had known him in Texas, made him his deputy.

Six months later, Carr resigned and Brown took over, naming Ben Wheeler from Rockdale, Texas, his deputy. The Caldwell citizens were pleased with their police force. They noted that Brown did not "drink, smoke, chew, or gamble." Some, however, wondered if Brown was too quick on the trigger.

In May, 1883, Brown shot and killed Spotted Horse, a Pawnee Indian, who had brought one of his wives to Caldwell for prostitution purposes. After the Indian and his wife had coerced the Long Branch Hotel into serving them breakfast, she went to their wagon to start work, and he went to a grocery store to extort food. Brown found Spotted Horse at the store, and the Indian woman no longer had either a husband or a pimp.

The citizens were pleased with the economics of the marshal's office. In August, 1883, Brown had collected $1296 in fines for the preceding five months, $421 more than the combined salaries of his office for the same period.

In December, 1883, a Texas gambler who had threatened Brown, slid his hand into his pocket, and Brown responded. The coroner's verdict was death at the hand of an officer in the discharge of his duties.

On March 27, 1884, Brown married; two weeks later the couple bought a house in Caldwell. Two weeks after that, Brown and Wheeler received permission from the citizens to leave town and hunt for a murderer in Indian Territory, for whom a reward was offered. Perhaps they needed extra money; Wheeler had been married three years, and he had a one-year-old child.

Instead of riding to Indian Territory, the peace officers picked up two Texas cowboys, Billy Smith and John Wesley who worked on ranches nearby, and they rode sixty miles northwest to Medicine Lodge. Early on April 30, 1884, they entered the town in a driving rain and tied their horses behind a coal shed at the rear of the Medicine Valley bank. When the bank opened its doors, three of the visitors walked in, leaving Billy Smith outside as a lookout.

Bank president, E. W. Payne was sitting at his desk, and cashier George Geppert was looking over the accounts. Brown called out that they were robbing the bank. Payne, a foolish man, reached into his desk drawer for a pistol, and Brown shot him. Geppert, a hero, ran to the open vault and closed and locked the door before Wheeler and Wesley shot him down. He died instantly; Payne died the next day.

The four would-be robbers ran through a hail of gunfire to reach their horses. They rode out of town with twenty men and the Medicine Lodge marshal hot on their heels. A few miles out of town, they turned into a narrow canyon and dismounted to fight on foot. The gun battle lasted two hours in the cold, drenching rain. The four men were standing in two feet of water when they surrendered to Sheriff C. F. Rigg.

The sheriff brought the prisoners to the jail in Medicine Lodge, but irate citizens demanded quicker justice. Brown wrote a letter to his new wife, giving it to the sheriff for delivery. He told her he was sorry for what happened. He only did it for the money and his love for her. "I thought we could take in the money and not have any trouble; but a man's fondest hopes are sometimes broken."

Shortly after dark, the citizens broke into the jail and overpowered the sheriff. The four prisoners tried to run. Brown was shot and killed; the other three were captured and taken to a large elm tree at the edge of town. Wheeler begged for mercy. The cowboys calmly told their captors their wishes about selling their property and sending the money to relatives in Texas. The three were quickly hanged.

When the citizens of Caldwell had given Brown his engraved rifle just sixteen months before, they described him as "cool, courageous, and gentlemanly and free from the vices usually found in such officers."

The citizens of Medicine Lodge certainly disagreed.

Suggested Reading: N. H. Miller & J. W. Snell, *Great Gunfighters of the Kansas Cowtowns* (Lincoln: Univ. of Neb. Press, 1967).

LOOKING FOR EXCITEMENT

Courage and skill with weapons were desirable qualities on both sides of the law in the Old West. Some men slipped from one side to the other with ease. Frank Canton, famous Wyoming sheriff, is a good example.

His real name was Joe Horner, born in Virginia in 1849. After their father, a Confederate surgeon, died of Civil War wounds, Joe and his brother moved the family to Texas.

When he was twenty, Joe trailed cattle to Abilene for Burk Burnett. He got his first law-related work in 1871 after Kiowa and Comanche Indians attacked a government wagon train near Jacksboro. The sheriff, recognizing Joe's courage and skill, hired him to escort Chiefs Satanta and Big Tree for their daily appearances in trial.

Joe stayed on in the cattle business. An occasional warrant for theft suggests that he relied on a long rope, as did some others starting that business. Finally, on October 10, 1874, Joe got into a shootout with off-duty black cavalrymen in a Jacksboro saloon. Leaving one soldier dead and another seriously wounded, Joe shot his way out of town and galloped north to Nebraska. He arrived there as Frank Canton, the name Joe Horner disappearing into history.

In 1878 Canton was a deputy sheriff in Custer County, Montana, and a field inspector for the Wyoming Stock Growers' Association. Two years later he moved to Johnson County, Wyoming, where he started his own ranch twelve miles south of Buffalo, and continued to work for the association. Two years after that he was elected county sheriff.

Canton presented an imposing figure. Tall and ramrod straight with piercing eyes, a handlebar mustache, and an authoritarian voice, he inspired respect in all and fear in most. His skill with horses and guns, added to his forceful personality, gave him the power needed to tame the unruly West.

Canton needed eighteen deputies to handle his huge county. Arrests of road agents, stage robbers, and rustlers cleaned up the county and brought Canton fame as an outstanding peace officer. His personal arrest of Teton Jackson, Wyoming's most dangerous and vicious badman, made him famous.

Re-elected in 1884, Canton soon had problems with Indian cattle rustlers. Remarkable detective work pointed to

FRANK CANTON

Western History Collections
University of Oklahoma Libraries

Samuel, a young Indian in Sharp Nose's band of Arapahoes. Canton rode into the middle of the enemy camp at midnight, grabbed the culprit, and outran his pursuers in a twenty-mile race to Fort Washakie. When Sharp Nose tried to prevent the arrest by grabbing Canton's bridle, Canton clubbed him down with his Winchester.

Canton retired in 1885 at the end of his second term. He was proud that in his four years he had served every criminal writ and indictment that he received. Not once did he report "not found."

The year before his retirement Canton had married Anna May Wilkerson, a talented musician, and they soon had a baby daughter. He decided to settle down to ranching. But the forces that led to the Johnson County War were building. Increasing losses of cattle to small ranchers and homesteaders drove the large ranchers in the Wyoming Stock Growers' Association to defensive measures.

When Frank Canton took sides it was not with the small ranchers and farmers who had twice elected him sheriff. He joined the cattle kings as chief detective for the Association and became the point man in a private war waged by wealth and power, supported by government, against ordinary citizens, most of whom had done nothing wrong.

On November 1, 1891, Canton and two other men burst into the cabin of Nate Champion, the cowboy the association most hated, and tried to kill him. Canton was released after a preliminary hearing in court.

On December 1, a bushwack murder a few miles from Canton's ranch seemed to be clearly tied to him. John Tisdale was driving a wagon to his ranch when he was shot in the back. The killer was seen leading Tisdale's team and his apparently empty wagon to a gulch, a short distance from the killing, where both horses were then shot. The witness, a neighboring rancher, recognized both the man and the horse he was riding. It was his friend, Frank Canton. The neighbor started to ride over and say hello when he saw Canton draw his gun. The neighbor rode on, minding his own business. In a few minutes he heard two shots — the shots that killed the horses.

In spite of that and other, less clear, evidence, Canton was released after his preliminary hearing and never came to trial. Later it was learned that Tisdale and Canton had known each other in Texas, and that Canton (or Horner as he was known then) had killed two of Tisdale's friends. Tisdale had also expressed a great fear of Canton a few days before his murder.

Canton never mentioned the Joe Horner part of his life in his autobiography, *Frontier Trails.* In that book he claims that Tisdale was killed by an unknown person.

The Johnson County war ended in a draw; the last move was the filing of *State of Wyoming vs. Frank Canton et al.* Most of the defendants fled the state; those that stayed got their cases dismissed by a friendly judge. Frank Canton spent a year of boredom in Nebraska and moved on to Oklahoma looking for excitement.

With the Doolin gang and other outlaws ravaging the territory, excitement abounded. Canton served here and there as deputy sheriff, sometimes deputy marshal. One of Canton's Oklahoma highlights was meeting Bill Dunn, one of the men Bill Tilghman had faced in the dungeon of death. Canton was serving summonses on jurors in Pawnee in 1896 when Dunn suddenly appeared before him, cursing, his hand on his revolver. Canton, hands in his pockets and a gun in his waistband, did not hesitate. He drew and shot Dunn between the eyes before the outlaw could shoot.

The next year Oklahoma Territory seemed too tame, so Canton went to Alaska, was appointed deputy United States Marshal, got caught up in the Klondike gold rush, and became a close friend of writer Rex Beach, with whom he prospected for gold. Canton also knew Owen Wister, another famous writer.

Snow blindness returned Canton to the United States in 1899. After treatment, his quest for excitement took him to China in a relief expedition to American troops in the Boxer Rebellion. Then he returned to Oklahoma and other peace officer appointments. After Oklahoma won statehood in 1907, Canton became its first adjutant general. He commanded Oklahoma's national guard until 1916.

When Canton died in 1927, rumors said that he was the model for Glenister, the main figure in the book, *The Spoilers,* written by his prospecting pal, Rex Beach. The movie based on the book starred John Wayne and Randolph Scott, and contains the longest and best fist fight in Hollywood history.

So who knows? Canton's life would surely have fit the part.

Suggested reading: William G. Bell, "Frontier Lawman" in *The American West* (Summer, 1964, Vol. 1, No. 3).

FAST GUN MARSHAL

David Neagle was thirty-three when he became a deputy
sheriff under Johnny Behan in Tombstone in 1881. Later that
year he succeeded Virgil Earp as marshal of Tombstone. His
career as an average Arizona lawman changed radically when
he became a U. S. marshal and got swept up in a whirlwind.

Neagle's reputation as one of the fastest pistol shots in
the West probably led to his selection as bodyguard for
Justice Stephen Field of the United States Supreme Court. In
that service Neagle would kill a former member of the
California Supreme Court.

It all started in 1849 when Texas lawyer David Terry
followed the gold rush to California. He practiced law in
Stockton and was elected to the state supreme court in 1855.

Field also came to California in the gold rush to settle in
Marysville. He was elected to the state supreme court in 1857.
By then Terry was chief justice.

Some of the conflict between these two supreme court
justices with giant egos probably had Civil War overtones.
Terry offered his services to Jefferson Davis as a general in the
Confederacy. Turned down, he fought anyway — apparently
without any rank — and was wounded. Field, from one of
America's most distinguished families of lawyers, was a
northerner, who would be named by President Lincoln to the
federal court.

But the whirlwind that enveloped Neagle began with
litigation between the United States Senator from Nevada and
his beautiful young mistress, who wanted more than her
fancy apartment in San Francisco's Palace Hotel. Sarah Hill
hired David Terry, by then back in private practice, to get her
a ring and a married name from Senator William Sharon.

The litigation took many years in both state and federal
courts. Much of the federal litigation was heard by Stephen
Field, as he made his California circuits.

The whirlwind increased in ferocity during a California
hearing in September, 1888. By this time Senator Sharon was
dead, and Terry, a widower, had married his client. Also the
enmity between Terry and Field had increased when Terry
refused to support Field in his try for the presidency four
years before.

At a tense point in the hearing, Sarah raised a fuss and
Field ordered the marshal (not Neagle) to lock her up. Before
the scene had ended, Terry had knocked the marshal across

the courtroom and had drawn a knife, proving his determination to protect his wife.

Field sentenced Sarah to thirty days for contempt of court, and he gave Terry six months. Threats made by both during their confinement led to Neagle being appointed bodyguard for Justice Field. Neagle knew that Terry had once killed one of California's U. S. senators, David Broderick, in a celebrated duel.

Early in the afternoon of August 13, 1889, Justice Field and Neagle boarded the train in Los Angeles to go to San Francisco. By coincidence David and Sarah Terry boarded the same train in Fresno at three in the morning, as they were to appear in court in San Francisco later that day. The train made a breakfast stop in Lathrop, just south of Stockton.

Justice Field and Neagle walked into the restaurant, sat down at the first table, and ordered. Terry and his wife came in shortly after. Sarah, seeing Field, wheeled around and left in a hurry. Terry took a seat at the next table.

One of the proprietors, seeing Sarah leave, went up to Terry. "I hope she's not so indiscreet as to get a pistol and cause a disturbance," he said.

"Why should she," Terry replied. "Who's here?"

Upon hearing Field's name, Terry looked disturbed and asked the proprietor to prevent Sarah from coming back in.

Then Terry got up, walked to Field's table and slapped his face twice. Neagle testified that he thought Terry was reaching for a knife, so he drew his gun and fired twice, shooting Terry through the heart.

The sheriff of Stanislaus County boarded the train and took Neagle into custody, although the killing had occurred in San Joaquin County. Neagle was not required to stand trial.

Public reaction was mixed. A Stockton newspaper reflected the community ambiguity: "Terry had a Bowie knife all the way from a foot to eighteen inches long, the blood of his last victim still on the blade. He picked his teeth with it while the Reverend Mr. Neagle, a distinguished prelate from Arizona entered the room on the arm of Stephen Field, a sacred personage descended from Heaven to execute the will of God upon earth."

In fact, Terry, although clearly a hothead, was unarmed.

Suggested reading: A. Russell Buchanan, *David S. Terry of California, Dueling Judge* (San Marino: The Huntington Library, 1956).

LAST OF THE OLD-TIME GUNFIGHTERS

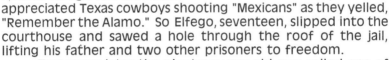

Residents of Socorro County, New Mexico, called Elfego Baca the best sheriff they ever had. Over fifty when elected, he took office with a long history on both sides of the law.

The history started in Socorro in 1882, when Elfego's father, the city marshal, had been jailed for killing two Texas cowboys who had been shooting up the town.

Baca ancestors had occupied the American southwest since before the Pilgrims reached Plymouth Rock, and neither Elfego nor his father appreciated Texas cowboys shooting "Mexicans" as they yelled, "Remember the Alamo." So Elfego, seventeen, slipped into the courthouse and sawed a hole through the roof of the jail, lifting his father and two other prisoners to freedom.

Two years later the nineteen-year-old was called one of the most courageous gunfighters in the West. That fall Elfego was working in Socorro when a friend, Deputy Sheriff Pedro Sarracino, said he was afraid to make arrests in Francisco (now Reserve, county seat of Catron County), because Texas cowboys controlled the town and scoffed at the law.

Sarracino then told of a native known as El Burro being stretched on a store counter by cowboys and "then and there alternated in the presence of everybody." When another native objected, he was tied to a tree and used for target practice. Elfego rode back to Francisco with Sarracino. Shortly after their arrival a cowboy shot up the town. Elfego asked the alcalde to issue a warrant so he could arrest the man.

"You go back to Socorro and mind your own business, if you want to keep your health," the alcalde suggested.

Elfego pinned on a tin mail-order badge and took the cowboy into custody. Elfego held no office. The badge meant as much as one we would get now from a cereal box. That evening the ranch foreman and more cowboys rode to town and demanded the release of their friend.

"I'll count to three to give you time to get out of town," Elfego replied.

He didn't hesitate between numbers, and he started shooting at "three." Only one cowboy got hit as they scattered for cover. But unfortunately the foreman's horse reared and fell, crushing its rider to death.

The next morning a justice of the peace agreed to try the wounded cowboy, then in custody. He found him guilty of disturbing the peace and fined him five dollars. By this time, the town was full of angry cowboys, determined to put down the "Mexican" rebellion. When he heard their first shot, Elfego sprinted down an alley, chased a woman and her children from their tiny *jacal* and jumped inside to hide.

Over eighty cowboys surrounded the one-room shack. Rancher Jim Herne battered on the door.

"Come out, you dirty little greaser," Herne shouted," or we'll drag you out."

Elfego, knowing he'd be hanged without benefit of law, answered with two shots into Herne's heart. Then began one of the most incredible one-man stands in history.

The *jacal*, made of upright poles chinked with mud, had large cracks between poles. A poorer place to withstand a siege could not be imagined. But the dirt floor was about a foot below ground level, and Elfego lay flat, rising from time to time to squeeze off a shot. Also, he could see his targets better in the bright sunlight than the grim cowboys could see theirs in the dark interior.

By evening, the cowboys wondered how Elfego could still be alive. They had tried to burn the roof, but its dirt covering saved it. They did throw dynamite which exploded, collapsing part of the roof.

By morning light the besieging army of cowboys saw the final touch of Elfego's personality. Smoke was rising from the dilapidated chimney. The nineteen-year-old youth was cooking breakfast! He had found coffee, enough beef for a stew, and had even made some tortillas.

As the second day wore on, some cowboys drifted away, claiming that Elfego had a charmed life, with immunity from bullets.

After thirty-six hours, Elfego agreed to surrender to a deputy sheriff he trusted. Even then he refused to give up his guns. After the details of the surrender agreement had been shouted back and forth, Elfego leaped out a window, his six-guns in his hands. Francisco natives shouted, "run, run," but Elfego knew that would give the Texans their excuse to shoot him down in the open. He surrendered to the deputy.

The cowboys estimated that thousands of bullets had poured into the shack. They counted nearly four hundred bullet holes in the door, eight in a broom handle. Elfego had not been scratched.

Even after arrest Elfego refused to give up his guns. The arresting deputy took him back to Socorro in a buckboard, but Elfego called the tune. The escort of six cowboys rode well out in front, keeping in plain sight, and Elfego watched from the back of the buckboard, his guns in his hands.

Elfego was tried for Herne's murder and acquitted. During the four months he spent in jail, he thought hard about his future. He decided to get married and study to become a lawyer, maybe even some day "a number one peace officer."

Elfego married at twenty. He and his wife had six children. He was admitted to the New Mexico bar at twenty-nine. He had a long productive career, both as a defense lawyer and as a district attorney. He was elected to several public offices.

During the 1910-1913 revolution in Mexico, General Huerta named Baca his American representative. During this time, Baca spent a lot of time in El Paso and Juarez. Celestino Otero, supporting a different Mexican faction, once agreed to meet Baca at an El Paso cafe. When Baca stepped out of his car, Otero fired, hitting Elfego in the groin. The old gunman still had his skill. He fired twice, hitting Otero both times in the heart. An El Paso jury acquitted Elfego.

In 1919, after two decades of spectacular law practice, Elfego Baca became sheriff of Socorro County. His first act was to gather up all the unserved arrest warrants and write a note to each wanted man, saying if he did not come in, the sheriff would come after him. All came but one, who challenged Elfego to meet him at a certain time and place. Elfego buckled on his guns and appeared at the place. The man, not there, was in the sheriff's office when Elfego returned.

"Shucks, Elfego," the wanted man said, "that was just a joke, just whisky talking in me."

In his old age, Elfego became a bouncer for the Tivoli, a famous night club in Juarez. During a time when Juarez night spots were being robbed on a regular basis, no one ever tried to rob the Tivoli with its old style gunman as bouncer.

Elfego Baca, unwilling to retire, returned to law practice in New Mexico. In summer 1945 a mushroom cloud in New Mexico ushered in the atomic age. Two months later the last of the old-time gunfighters, who had lived his life disdaining fear in any form, died quietly at age eighty.

Suggested reading: Jack Schaefer, *Heroes Without Glory* (Boston: Houghton Mifflin, 1965).

COLD TRAIL IN ARIZONA

Sheriff Buckey O'Neill of Yavapai County, Arizona Territory,. had his shoes up on his desk when the telegraph agent barged in.

"They held up the express at Canyon Diablo," the agent announced. "They think it was four cowboys from the Hashknife outfit." He showed his telegram to Buckey.

Buckey jumped to his feet and grabbed his hat.

"What are you going to do?" the agent asked.

"Get a posse and get after them."

"Hell, they'll have three days start by the time you get there. Cold trailing in that rough country is a losing proposition."

"I'll give it a try."

It was March 20, 1889, and everybody knew the robbers would head north for Utah. District Attorney H. D. Ross told Buckey to forget about it. The robbers only got $1300 in money and jewels, and the sheriff had no authority outside his county. The chairman of the county supervisors refused to authorize deputies for an illegal chase.

"If they left the county it's a capital offense," Buckey replied, "and it's my job as sheriff to bring them in."

Buckey got new shoes on his big roan, Sandy, laid in a huge supply of food and Bull Durham tobacco, and picked up Cal Holton, special agent for the railroad, and special deputies Ed St. Clair and Jim Black. They headed for Canyon Diablo the next day.

The trail was cold as a corpse. The rocky ground was frozen hard, and sleet had eliminated any sign of a hoof print. They found ashes of an old fire by the right of way. An occasional scar on a stone, a broken twig, horsehair snarled on a bush, an overturned pebble showed that the robbers had headed south. Then they found where precious stones had been pried out of jewelry, and the trail seemed to swing north.

"I knew it," Buckey said. "Let's ride for Utah."

After a night on the trail, they rode into Black Falls on the Little Colorado River. No one had seen the outlaws. But Buckey had cut sign all along and he was sure the chase had grown warmer.

"Lee's Ferry is the only place they can cross the Colorado," he said. "Let's head them off there."

They galloped across the Painted Desert, Buckey's Sandy far in the lead. But the other horses could not keep up, and they were two days behind the robbers at Lee's Ferry.

When the posse reached Cannonville, Utah, the Mormons, suspicious of any outside peace officers, said they had seen no fugitives. In fact, they had not, as Buckey had led his posse on a six hundred mile chase in ten days, reaching Cannonville twelve hours ahead of the outlaws. The posse headed southwest to Pahreah, hoping to find their fugitives there.

When they reached Pahreah a messenger from Cannonville said the outlaws had been captured there. Disappointed that he had not made the capture himself but glad to get the fugitives, Buckey led his posse back to Cannonville.

But the outlaws had escaped their Mormon captors by the time Buckey arrived. "Guess we'll keep riding," the determined sheriff said.

After a furious gun battle on a rocky point overlooking Wah Weep Canyon, as isolated from civilization today as it was then, Buckey captured two of the fugitives, John Halford and Bill Stiren. He told Black and St. Clair to take the prisoners to Kanab, while he and Cal Holton continued after the other two.

After another gun battle, Buckey and Holton captured the remaining two men, J. J. Smith and Dan Harvick.

But the battle was only half won. Buckey had to get the prisoners back to Prescott. He was deep in a wilderness which, still today, defies exploration. They rode northwest to Milford, where Buckey sent a wire to Prescott that he had his men, the first public news since Buckey had left twenty days before. The posse and its prisoners rode the train to Salt Lake City, where Buckey was able to get irons for his prisoners.

They rode east to Denver and took another train south. As the train slowed to climb Raton Pass, Black and Holton stood watch while Buckey and St. Clair slept. Smith slipped out of his leg irons and jumped out the window to escape.

Buckey returned to Prescott with his three prisoners, leaving Black and Holton in New Mexico to look for Smith. Congratulatory telegrams from all over the West flooded into Prescott on Buckey's capture. The three men pleaded guilty and got twenty-five years each. Smith was captured by the Vernon, Texas, sheriff and returned. He got thirty years.

Buckey had spent $8200 in the pursuit. The county refused to pay $2300 of it, saying it was spent outside Yavapai County, where Buckey had no authority. Buckey sued the county for the unpaid amount.

The judge waxed eloquently in describing how Buckey and his rough riders had successfully pursued the worst freebooters since Roderic Dhu of Scotland and Robin Hood of England had ravaged those countries. "Across vast sandy plains, up and over rugged mesas and mountains, through cañons and mountain gorges the pursuit is waged, until at last they are overtaken, a fight ensues, and they are captured. But since it is over the Utah line, it is contended the sheriff can get nothing for his magnificent work."

Defying state law and centuries of precedent, the judge ruled for Buckey. But the district attorney appealed to the state supreme court, which reversed, leaving Buckey holding the bag for his out-of-state expenses.

Even though Yavapai County at that time was larger than the state of Indiana, Buckey must have had a creative accountant to justify his division between in-state and out-of-state expenses.

Buckey ran twice for congress, both times unsuccessfully, and then became mayor of Prescott. He joined the 1st U. S. Volunteer Cavalry (Rough Riders) as a private at the start of the Spanish-American War. He had risen to be captain of A Troop when they shipped out for Cuba.

On July 1, 1898, Buckey walked up and down in front of his line of men waiting for the signal to charge up San Juan Hill. With bullets whizzing all about him, someone shouted, "Take it easy, captain. You'll be killed sure."

"The Spanish bullet with my name on it hasn't been molded yet," Buckey replied.

But as he turned, a bullet entered his mouth and came out at the back of his head. Colonel Theodore Roosevelt lauded the man as he was buried in Arlington National Cemetery. "He quoted Whitman on the field of battle, and he fought all his gutsy life against injustice to the weak. He loved a row as a schoolboy does a holiday. His life work is written deep in a territory redeemed from lawlessness."

Roosevelt was right. Train robbing continued in Arizona, but not again in Yavapai County while Buckey O'Neill was sheriff.

Suggested reading: Ralph Keithley, *Buckey O'Neill* (Caldwell, Idaho: The Caxton Printers, 1949).

LONG HAIRED SHARPSHOOTER

The parents of Commodore Perry Owens must have admired a naval hero when they named their son. But his fame rested neither on his unusual name nor on his long hair. It came from courage and incredible shooting skill.

He drifted into Arizona with its first stage line and became a horse herder at the Navajo Springs station in 1882. His constant warfare with Navajos started with his fighting horse thieves. A tall man with a high nose and piercing gray eyes, he wore his hair long as a standing invitation to the Navajos to come and get it if they could. They never could.

Once, a large band tried to intercept and ambush him as he rode toward a pass. Owens, who raised and rode the best blooded horses in Arizona, beat them to the pass, but, instead of riding on through to safety, he dismounted and waited for them to ride up. He killed four or five before the others got away.

Owens turned to ranching near Cottonwood. That part of Arizona was a crossroads of hostility where Mexicans fought Anglos, whites fought Indians, cattlemen fought sheepman, locals fought Texans, and only the Mexicans tried to exercise authority.

Owens once walked alone into a building where eighty Mexican deputies held two Texans prisoner. Drawing his pistol, Owens asked the prisoners what they were doing in the building.

"Just sitting around," they answered.

"Well, you come out right now."

There was no trouble, not a single Mexican protest. Their Mexican posse rode on empty-handed. That day marked a turning point in Texan - Mexican hostility. From then on, Texans and their cattle flooded into the valley. The Mexicans were glad to keep to the hills, raising sheep. This is when the large Hashknife outfit, the Aztec Land and Cattle Company, got its start.

Soon after this, a shoot-out in Holbrook gave the Bucket of Blood saloon its name, and the Grahams and Tewksburys started their feud which led to the Pleasant Valley War. In an attemt to keep order, Navajo County was formed with Holbrook the county seat; Owens was elected sheriff.

Owens took no sides. The long-haired lawman walked the streets, two .45 caliber six-shooters at his belt. He also kept a .45-60 Sharps, sighted to shoot a mile, and a lighter, magazine rifle for closer work. He carried both when mounted, only the lighter one when afoot. He had no courthouse and no jail, and most of the county's citizens were fugitives from justice. Entitled to deputies, he rode alone — probably because he had no one to trust.

Owens once pursued a man outide his county into the Tonto Basin, where the Pleasant Valley war was raging. He lost the man and was on his way out when a messenger rode up, saying Old Man Blevens would kill him if he ever again entered the basin. The fighting cattlemen and sheepmen had bragged that no officer dared ride into their valley.

Owens turned around immediately and rode to Blevens headquarters. They fired on him from cover. When Owens rode away, he left the old man and two of his sons behind, dead. He had shot the last one after kicking the door open and bursting into the gunsmoke-filled interior.

In neighboring Winslow a faro dealer shot at a Mexican in an argument over cards. He missed, but the Mexican, while slower, was more accurate, killing the dealer. The gambler was popular and Mexicans were not. A lynch mob quickly formed.

In the meantime the Mexican surrendered to Owens. The mob demanded that he release the man to them.

"There aren't enough of you," Owens said. "To get him you'll have to kill me."

The mob faded away.

Owens was drawn back into the Pleasant Valley war, and the result was the most remarkable quick shooting in the history of the West. Four from the Blevens side were holed up in a house in Holbrook, and Owens had a warrant for one of them. He walked up to the house and demanded that his man come outside. In the next few seconds the wanted man fired his gun through the door and two others burst out, also shooting at Owens. Firing the rifle from his hip, without taking time to raise it to his shoulder, Owens dropped all three, two dead and one wounded.

Only the youngest Blevens boy, aged sixteen, was still in the house with his mother. He started out, but his mother tried to drag him back. She pleaded with Owens to not shoot.

"Ma'am, a boy can pull a trigger just as hard as a man," he warned.

The boy broke free and started to shoot. Owens dropped him, dead, with one shot. The Pleasant Valley war was over.

But killing the boy bothered Owens. He resigned, had his hair cut short and went back to his ranch. He married, raised a family, and lived long in the land he had cleared from outlaws with his quick, accurate guns.

Suggested reading: Dane Coolidge, *Fighting Men of the West* (New York: E. P. Dutton & Co., 1932).

A BAD MORNING ALL AROUND

Western gunfights came in three models: man against man, posse against gang, and, sometimes, town against town. The county seat wars came in the third category. The 1889 battle between Ingalls and Cimarron to be county seat of Gray County in southwestern Kansas provides an example.

The dispute in Gray County led to the voters of Foote Township offering to sell their block of seventy votes to either side for seven thousand dollars. Ingalls turned them down; Cimarron said they would pay after the election results were final. Foote Township citizens didn't care who won.

Cimarron won the election, but the court invalidated it for fraud, declaring Ingalls the county seat. Sheriff Bill Tilghman was ordered to move the county records from Cimarron to Ingalls. He deputized seven men to recover the records, and hired two teamsters with wagons to haul them.

The streets were deserted that January 12, 1889, morning when the wagons entered Cimarron. Tilghman sent George Bolds, Jim and Tom Masterson, and two other deputies into the County Clerk's office to get the records. Jake Shoup, chairman of the county board of supervisors, was waiting inside, ready to shoot. His friend, Deputy George Bolds, out drew him.

"If you pull your gun, I'll shoot it out of your hand," Bolds said.

"I should have killed you when you were here last," Shoup replied.

Bolds disarmed Shoup, tied his hands, and rolled him under a chair so he wouldn't get hit if any gunfire broke out. Then five deputies started carrying out record books while another stood guard. The firing started on their second trip. A load of buckshot raked the building just above Bolds' head, as he came out with a load of books. The advancing Cimarron citizens — at least sixty strong, including two women — were shooting their way as they dodged from building to building.

"For God's sake, don't kill anybody," shouted Tilghman. "Get their horses, men — try to scare them off."

One of the Ingalls teamsters went down, shot in the hip. Screams of wounded horses sounded above the roar of rifles and six-shooters.

Bonds was hit in the leg, then in the neck. He and another

deputy got their wagon to the depot to join the other wagon and its deputies. But Jim and Tom Masterson and Neal Brown were not with them. By this time another deputy had been wounded, and they decided to pull out for Ingalls with their wagonloads of records.

They piled county ledgers and books into hasty barricades across the backs of the wagons and began a wild chase across the prairie, pursued by Cimarron citizens.

When they reached Ingalls, the wagon boxes and the blood-smeared county records books had been perforated, and Bonds had another wound in his leg. Blood dripped out of the wagons, as though they had been hauling butchered hogs. The teamsters pulled their heaving horses to a stop, and three wounded men were hurried to a doctor.

Meanwhile, back in Cimarron, the Mastersons and Brown were barricaded on the second floor of a building. Jake Shoup, freed from his bonds in the clerk's office, advanced carrying a white flag.

"Billy English is dead and we got some wounded, too," Shoup said. "There's enough blood been spilled."

"You should of thought of that before firing on peace officers," Jim Masterson said. "Did the rest of our men get away?"

"George Bolds is in a bad way and some others hit. It was a bad morning all around."

The three deputies came down to the street, their guns drawn, but no one opened fire. The strange procession moved to the depot. The three deputies were surrounded by grim, armed men, many of them their friends and acquaintances, ready to fire on the least provocation.

News of the battle had been telegraphed out of Cimarron. Bat Masterson, running a Denver gambling hall, had heard the news and sent this telegram back to Cimarron: If you don't let my brothers, both sworn peace officers, out of town peacefully, I'll hire a train and come in to Cimarron with enough men to blow it off the Kansas map.

Another Cimarron man died from his wounds, leaving two dead and several wounded in the strange war. But Cimarron wasn't ready to quit. Armed men began gathering in the town square, determined to burn Ingalls to the ground. Ingalls citizens built roadblocks and piled sandbags on their roofs. A posse from Dodge City rode to Ingalls to help its defense. The governor sent troops, who surrounded Cimarron and stayed until passions cooled. The war had finally ended.

Suggested reading: James D. Horan, *Across the Cimarron* (New York: Bonanza Books, 1956).

THE MYSTERIOUS DEPUTY

William Howard enjoyed many reminiscences before he died at ninety-seven. He was the last survivor of the California Rangers, a select company of the twenty best frontiersmen in the state during the gold rush. Their mission was to capture dreaded bandit Joaquin Murieta, dead or alive. They killed Murieta as well as his principal lieutenant, Three Fingered Jack. Then Howard went back to raising horses in the Sierra foothills. Soon he was the leading breeder and trainer of racehorses in the state.

Howard's earlier memories included hearing President Sam Houston, a frequent visitor to the Howard home in Texas, as Houston talked about getting his nation annexed to the United States. They included his service in the war against Mexico and his moving on to California, looking for gold.   They also included a   close friendship with David Terry, law school classmate in Texas, who became Chief Justice of California and later killed one of California's senators in a notorious duel. Finally, they included Howard's own public service in the California legislature and as a deputy sheriff in Mariposa County.   Perhaps his most interesting memories came from one case he solved as a sheriff's deputy when he was sixty years old.

Howard's frontier life in Texas and California fitted him well to be a typical western lawman — willing to stand his ground and shoot it out with anyone.   He once killed a man in an argument over land.   The jury said it was self defense.   But Howard's fame as a sheriff came from his detective work. Very soon it became clear that he had special talents — psychic powers they said. People called him the mysterious deputy.

In early 1886 a beautiful French woman moved to Mariposa County from Nevada. She wore expensive jewelry and said her name was Thelma Savageau. She met a French man, Louis Hebert, who had come west in the gold rush and turned sheepherder after losing interest in mining.   By this time Hebert was a prosperous Mariposa County rancher with a fondness for the bottle.   He spent much time in town, drinking.   Soon Hebert was infatuated with Thelma.   She moved in when he agreed to make her sole heir to his ranch. Then Thelma's husband, Peter, appeared. Strangely, he made no objection to the arrangement between Thelma and Hebert.

One morning in December 1886, without knowing why,

Howard warned Hebert to watch Peter Savageau, saying the man might try to kill him. Hebert assured Howard he could look out for himself. That night Howard had a vivid dream in which he saw Savageau shoot Hebert, cut the flesh away from the body, feed it to hogs, and burn the skeleton in a furnace.

The next day, unable to stop thinking about the dream, Howard looked around town to see if Hebert had showed up for his usual drinks. Later that day he told the sheriff, the district attorney, and the judge about his dream; he predicted they would never see Hebert again. The others scoffed and said Howard must have been drinking, himself, to have such a dream.

But the scoffers watched anxiously as three days passed with no sign of Hebert. Then Savageau and Thelma came to town with a wagon to haul the rest of Thelma's possessions out to the ranch. When asked about Hebert, Savageau said the man had left the county to go back to herding sheep.

Howard reminded the district attorney of his dream, and he bet him he would have Hebert's bones back in town within three hours. He rode quickly to the ranch, while Savageau and Thelma continued to load their wagon. Howard went directly to the furnace he had seen in his dream. He found Hebert's skull in the ashes. He returned to town with the evidence, collected his bet, and arrested Savageau.

That evening in the jail, Howard asked Savageau why he did not burn up the skull as he had the rest of the bones.

"My God, where's the head?" asked Savageau.

"Right outside."

"Why, I piled enough wood on it to burn a dozen heads," replied Savageau.

Savageau then confessed the crime. The details of the murder were exactly like Howard's dream, and he had killed Hebert at the very time Howard had the dream. Savageau was found guilty and sentenced to San Quentin Prison for life.

Howard's reputation as the mysterious deputy was still intact.

Suggested reading: Jill L. Cossley-Batt, *The Last of the California Rangers* (New York, Funk & Wagnalls, 1928).

THE MOUNTIES MOVE WEST

Canadian Fred Bagley, fifteen, dreamed of finding adventure in the West. He was an avid fan of James Fenimore Cooper novels, and his heart sung when he learned in 1874 that the Northwest Mounted Police were enlisting men in Toronto. The Mounties would provide the life for him!

"How old are ye, son?" the doctor asked after peeking, probing, and poking into Fred's skinny body.

"Eighteen, sir."

"Aye, and it's Queen Victoria, I am. Well, off with you anyway." He wrote in Fred's file: Very young, but may develop.

Colonel George French, the commander of the new brigade, had been an Imperial Army comrade of Fred's father, so one more hurdle remained.

"George won't worry about your age," Fred's father assured him, "but I've got some advice for you."

He told the boy about men in dark countries being lured into indiscretions by savages. After describing the horrors of volcanic sores, terrible swellings, and the agony of urination, he concluded, "You don't want to carry it around in a wheelbarrow, son. No matter how tempted you are, just keep it in your pants."

On June 6, with Cooper's *The Last of the Mohicans* in his pocket, Fred Bagley headed west, the youngest sub constable in the 300-man brigade. He was assigned to D Troop as assistant trumpeter.

Fred was no shirker, but there was always work to be done and he tired of "Lad, this," and "Lad, that," followed by someone else's idea of work that needed to be done right now. Even the half-bloods seemed to have more status than he. But he learned to make an easy job last and to become invisible between them. He knew he was being picked on, but the excitement of marching west to pacify hostile Indians and destroy whiskey traders was worth it.

Horses were issued to the troops at Fort Dufferin on the Red River, just north of the International boundary. Fred, an excellent horseman, didn't expect much, but what he got still shocked him. It was the slowest, ugliest nag Fred had ever seen. How could he rescue an Indian maiden on a horse that groaned loudly when spurred out of a slow trot? Something had to be done, and quickly!

Fred learned that the horses had not yet been officially recorded to their riders, and he planned a quick and creative move. But just as he located a spirited black issued to an inattentive trooper, he also learned that horses would be issued to troops by color. E Troop would get black ones, and Fred's D Troop would get grays and mustangs, a miscellaneous category that included buckskins, roans, and duns.

In a few days Fred saw a drunk man in B Troop holding a nice looking buckskin, as he watched a parade. Fred loaned him the money for another drink and offered to hold his horse while the drunk went for it.

"Shanks," the man said. "Damn horsheeves all around."

Fred felt some sympathy for his victim, but he knew there would be no complaint; the man wouldn't want to explain how he got in the position to lose his horse.

The D Troop commander, Captain James Walsh, saw Fred leading his new horse back to camp. "What's that you got there, lad?" he asked.

"Found him, sir. Wandering on the prairie, he was, sir."

"Sure. With your bridle, blanket and saddle on him, I see." He stepped closer to Fred, giving the horse a quick inspection and nodding his approval. "Is there going to be trouble over this?"

"No, sir." Fred snapped to attention.

"Well, book him in, then. He's yours."

A few days later the brigade started west toward that den of iniquity nine hundred miles away, Fort Whoop-Up and its whiskey traders. They skirted the Turtle Mountains, scene of a recent Indian attack on two half-blood families. Apparently most of the horses issued to sub constables resembled Fred's first mount. On July 19, as they were crossing the Souris River loop, Colonel French ordered the sub constables to alternate between riding one hour and walking one hour.

They saw their first Sioux in August on Old Wives Creek in present Saskatchewan. But there were only seven lodges, about thirty persons, and the Indians only wanted to talk.

They saw their first buffalo in early September in the Cypress Hills. The elation of shooting the beasts and feasting on fresh meat gave way to depression when they realized they were lost and could not find Fort Whoop-Up. One man, Sub Constable Thornton, demanded an immediate discharge.

"I joined this force to fight for Queen and country," he said. "So far I've only fought hunger, thirst, and cooties."

Thornton was sent to the doctor for a mental examination.

With the help of Jerry Potts, a half-blood guide, they found Fort Whoop-Up, but the whiskey traders were long gone.

With winter coming on, Colonel French divided his force into four parts. One moved west and built Fort McLeod, the first Mountie post in western Canada. One went north to Fort Edmonton. Another went northeast to Fort Pelly, found it uninhabitable, and built barracks on Swan River. The fourth, including Fred's D Troop, returned east to Fort Garry (present Winnipeg).

By this time the men were all in rags. Most had no soles on their shoes or wrapped their feet in gunny sack bindings. When D Troop stopped at Hudson's Bay Fort Qu Appelle, one man from each tent was sent to the fort for tobacco. Each emissary fitted himself out with the most presentable clothing in his tent. At this time they learned that newspapers had reported the whole brigade wiped out by hostile Indians. Prayers for their souls were being repeated in all of eastern Canada's churches.

That winter, mutinies had to be put down at three of the troop locations. The men had not been paid since leaving Fort Dufferin the previous July. Several deserted at Fort McLeod. Only lack of money kept others from following them south to the United States.

In April, the Fort Garry men learned that two men at Fort McLeod had frozen to death while on patrol three months before. By that time the Fort Garry men were eating bread and pork three times a day. They called the pork — rainbow colored with various shades of green — rattlesnake or three-foot pork. Fred was able, once in a while, to kill a rabbit.

Apparently Fred followed his father's advice. He married Lucy May Kerr-Francis in 1890, and they had six daughters. His career in the Mounties lasted just over twenty-five years. He was discharged a major at age forty-one. He had served fourteen years before he first saw his family after leaving Toronto.

After retirement Fred served in the Boer War and the first World War. He kept his trumpet, and late in life was conductor of the Calgary Citizens band.

At a reunion in the 1920s, Fred saw the man from whom he had stolen the buckskin.

"You son-of-a-gun," the man said, extending his hand.

"I hope you enjoyed the drink. Where's my fifty cents?"

The buckskin had been humanely put down in 1898, owing to its great age. Fred died in 1945, age eighty-seven.

Suggested reading: David Cruise and Alison Griffiths, *The Great Adventure* (New York: St. Martin's Press, 1996).

NORTHWEST MOUNTED POLICE BAND, BANFF, ALBERTA

Fred Bagley holding dog

Glenbow Archives, Calgary, Alberta

FOUR-EYED DEPUTY WITH SAND IN HIS CRAW

When Theodore Roosevelt visited his ranch in the North Dakota badlands in March, 1886, he learned that Wilmot Dow had recently killed four deer and hung their bodies in a thicket to keep them from coyotes. Dow and his uncle, Will Sewall, had been Roosevelt's eastern friends and western hunting companions, and were now managers of his ranch. The three men headed down the Little Missouri River in the ranch boat to bring the meat in.

Mountain lions had mangled the meat, leaving little but skin scraps and bones. Roosevelt resolved to kill the lions. They returned to the ranch to get a tracking dog and start after the lions the next day.

But that night their boat was stolen. All evidence pointed to Mike Finnigan, who had been living twenty miles upstream with two other hard characters, Dutch Pfaffenbach and Half-breed Burnsted. Local ranchers had been threatening to lynch Finnigan for his rustling. Besides leaving a tell-tale mitten at the scene, Finnigan, with a motive to leave the country, had the only other boat on the river and it was a poor one. Roosevelt's boat was sound. Fleeing downstream while the river was flooding between banks jammed with ice was a good bet for escape. There were no doubts about who took the boat.

Following the thieves down the little-explored stream, gorged with ice and in the wildest part of the badlands, while expecting an ambush at any moment, would make most men think twice. But Theodore Roosevelt wasn't like most men.

Once he had confronted a deputy U. S. Marshal who was holding a gun against his stomach.

"Shoot and be damned," Roosevelt had said. "You pledged your honor to uphold the law, and you're in league with the crooks."

The marshal, who was, in fact, acting improperly, backed down.

Another time in a saloon in Mingusville (present Wibaux, Montana); a bully had pointed both his guns at Roosevelt, saying, "Four-eyes is gonna treat." Roosevelt struck him three times and knocked him out. When the bully came to, he slipped down to the railroad station and left town on a freight.

Roosevelt's daring during a night cattle stampede had once led a ranch foreman to say, "That four-eyed maverick's got sand in his craw aplenty."

Outraged that someone would steal his property, Roosevelt had Sewall build a flat-bottomed scow large enough for the three men and their supplies. The supplies included a copy of Tolstoy's *Anna Karenina,* which Roosevelt brought along to read.

They had to wait three days for a furious blizzard to blow itself out before they started their down-river pursuit. On March 30 they slid their scow into the icy current. Each man carried a rifle, and they had a double-barrelled shotgun in reserve. Sewall and Dow, both rivermen from Maine, moved the scow through the ice. Their passenger, wrapped in a buffalo robe, read his novel.

All day they poled and drifted north through bleak, awesome country, facing the biting north wind. Sometimes the walls of ice towered ten feet above the boat. That night they camped on shore and the cold grew more intense. They piled furs on their blankets and slept fitfully, as ice floes in the river crunched and roared like a giant serpent writhing in pain.

At the end of their second day, the handles of their poles were encased in ice. That night the temperature dropped to zero.

The next afternoon, when they were about a hundred miles downstream from the ranch, they saw the stolen boat moored against the bank. Nearby, campfire smoke curled upward through the frozen air.

Pfaffenbach was alone in camp; his companions had gone hunting. He was captured and then placed by the fire as a decoy. Three guns trained on him forced his compliance.

Burnsted arrived next. They disarmed him and hid him along the bank and waited for Finnigan.

A half hour later Finnigan approached. Roosevelt jumped up and ordered him to drop his rifle. Finnigan had once shot up the town of Medora after a wild drunk. It looked for a moment that Finnigan would start shooting now. But Roosevelt stepped closer, shoving his rifle against Finnigan's chest. The thief surrendered.

But now the cold would test the endurance of Roosevelt and his men, as much as their courage had been tested before. Tied up, the prisoners would freeze to death. They had to be guarded around the clock.

To complicate matters, the men were stopped the next day by an ice jam. Roosevelt found little amusement in the

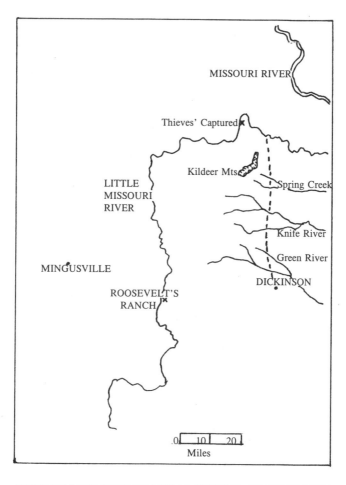

MISSOURI RIVER

Thieves' Captured

Kildeer Mts.

Spring Creek

LITTLE
MISSOURI
RIVER

Knife River

Green River

MINGUSVILLE

DICKINSON

ROOSEVELT'S
RANCH

0 10 20
Miles

DEPUTY ROOSEVELT'S PURSUIT OF THIEVES

combined life of a sheriff and an arctic explorer. They had planned to float on down the river another thirty miles to the nearest ranch. They struggled six days through the ice jam to reach an out-lying cow camp of the C Diamond ranch. By that time they had consumed practically all their food and were down to flour mixed with river water.

Roosevelt borrowed a horse and rode fifteen miles to reach a ranch in the Killdeer Mountains. There he arranged to hire a wagon and a team. He returned to the river and walked the prisoners to the ranch. On April tenth he said goodbye to Dow and Sewall, who returned to the boats and continued down the river and the Missouri River to Mandan.

Roosevelt hired a man to drive the wagon to Dickinson. Knowing nothing about the man he hired, Roosevelt was afraid to let the prisoners or the driver get too close to him. So he walked behind the wagon, his rifle at the ready.

That night they reached an abandoned shack. Roosevelt put the driver in the lower bunk and all three prisoners in the upper one. He spent the night on the floor, his back to the door, his eyes open, his rifle ready.

The weather warmed, but a cold, misty rain fell all the next day. Roosevelt slogged behind the wagon in the mud. When they crossed the headwaters of the Knife and Green Rivers the ice had piled so high along the banks, they had to dismantle the wagon to get through.

When Roosevelt turned his prisoners over to the sheriff in Dickinson he had walked over forty miles during thirty-six hours without sleep. This came after the previous eleven days of fighting ice in the river. He was still indignant that anyone would steal his property.

Roosevelt had been a member of the New York state assembly. He would later be a military hero in the Spanish-American War and president of the United States. Apparently he never held an official title as a law enforcer. However, under the laws of Dakota Territory he did collect a deputy sheriff's pay, including mileage. For three arrests and about three hundred miles traveled — boat, horse, and on foot — he got fifty dollars.

And Dakota Territory got a bargain! The thieves probably welcomed the warmth and quiet of the territorial prison with no four-eyed guards ordering them around.

Suggested reading: Carleton Putnam, *Theodore Roosevelt, the Formative Years* (New York: Charles Scribner's Sons, 1958).

WELLS FARGO DETECTIVE

Jim Hume left an Indiana farm for California in 1850. Ten years of prospecting brought little success, so he became a deputy sheriff in El Dorado County and then city marshal of Placerville in 1862. Two years later, as undersheriff for the county, he brought to justice the robbers in one of the West's most bizarre stage holdups.

A band of Confederate sympathizers had held up two stages on the road from Lake Bigler (Tahoe) to Placerville. The leader said they needed the bullion to raise troops for the South. The fleeing bandits killed an officer to whom Hume was close. "Frantic with grief and rage," Jim relentlessly hunted down the whole band. From then on, Jim seemed obsessed with bringing criminals to justice.

In 1873, after Jim had solved some important cases and had served as deputy warden of the Nevada State Prison, he became chief detective for Wells Fargo. Forty-six at the time, he served the company for thirty more years, becoming the West's most legendary detective.

Of all the stage robbers brought to justice by Jim Hume — Dick Fellows, the Ruggles Brothers, Evans and Sontag, Louis Dreibelbis, the most famous was Black Bart.

Charles Boles, a New Yorker who moved to San Francisco, started stage robbing in 1875 when he was about forty-three. He always worked alone, generally disguised with a flour-sack hood over his head. In twenty-eight holdups, he came away empty handed only once.

No one had any idea who the hooded man was. He started in the foothills east of San Francisco on the Sonora-Milton stage line. On July 26, 1875, as John Shine drove the stage up from the Stanislaus River toward Copperopolis, he heard the polite command, "Please throw down the box."

Shine later became a United States marshal and a California state senator. But on that day, as he looked into the double-barreled shotgun, he quickly complied. When a passenger threw out her purse, Black Bart politely returned it, saying he only wanted Wells Fargo's treasure.

Even though Bart often wore socks over his shoes to avoid leaving tracks, it seemed that he deliberately left clues to taunt Wells Fargo detectives. One time he left a note: "Driver, give my respects to our old friend, the other driver."

Then he started leaving poetry, signed Black Bart, the Po8. On his fifth robbery — in July, 1878 — he sat beside the road the day before the robbery so the driver would have a good look at him. Right after the holdup, the officers found this:

>Here I lay me down to sleep
>To await the coming morrow
>Perhaps success, perhaps defeat
>And everlasting sorrow.
>
>I've labored long and hard for bred
>For honor and for riches
>But on my corns too long you've tred
>You fine haired Sons of Bitches.
>
>Let come what will, I'll try it on
>My condition can't be worse
>And if there's money in that box
>"Tis munny in my purse.

By now, although no one had any idea of Black Bart's identity, Hume had pieced together a picture of his work habits. His boot size was eight, he always worked alone and on foot, he was a fast walker, and, although he usually waved a shotgun, he never fired it. (Hume would learn later that he never loaded it.)

Hume guessed correctly that when he was waiting between holdups, Bart liked to lose himself among the crowds in San Francisco. In fact, Bart loved the city streets. He dressed with elegance, favoring a derby, a tweed suit, a stylish cravat with diamond stickpin, and a velvet-collared overcoat.

Bart worked all over northern California, from the foothills to the northern mines and back to the north and south coasts. No one could anticipate where he would strike next.

Bart's luck ran out on Nov. 3, 1883. Ironically, he had decided to stage his twenty-eighth holdup at the same place he had held the first one. This time the Sonora-Milton stage was driven by Reason McConnell. As he pulled up from the Stanislaus River toward Copperopolis, he heard the polite command. But this time a ferryman, hitching a ride up from the Stanislaus to do some hunting, took a shot at the bandit, wounding him in the hand. In Bart's hurried departure with the loot, he left behind some articles, including a handkerchief.

Jim Hume, quickly on the scene, saw a laundry mark on the handkerchief. Six months earlier Jim had hired Harry

Morse, former sheriff of Alameda County, solely to help find Black Bart.

"Check out that mark, Harry," Hume said, handing over the handkerchief. "Maybe we finally got something that will locate him."

Morse starting calling on the ninety-one laundries in San Francisco. Eight days later he had nothing but disappointment and aching feet. But then he walked into Ferguson and Bigg's laundry, and they sent him to a tobacco shop on Post street, one of their agents who used the questioned mark.

When Morse found Black Bart he noticed how well the man fit the profile prepared by Jim Hume. Boles, who used the name Charles Bolton in his San Francisco life, played ignorant. Morse took him to the Wells Fargo headquarters in San Francisco to meet Hume. Bart did not bat an eye as he met, for the first time, his old adversary.

After lengthy verbal sparring between the insouciant bandit and the indefatigable detective, Hume took Bart to his room and searched it.

"What right have you to search?" demanded Bart.

Hume did not answer, but he found a handkerchief with the same mark. He also found poetry matching that left at the holdup scenes. He had enough. He arrested Black Bart.

After visits to local jails for identification and hours of intensive questioning, Black Bart finally confessed. He pleaded guilty to the last holdup and got six years in San Quentin.

Released in 1888 after four years in prison, Black Bart soon disappeared from California. Hume, who had married four years before, continued as Wells Fargo's chief detective. He was heavily involved in the 1890s in California's undeclared civil war when the Southern Pacific Railroad fought an alliance of farmers and small businessmen, supported by reformers such as Adolph Sutro and Frank Norris. Wells Fargo was a virtual satellite of the powerful railroad monopoly in that war.

Advancing age forced Jim Hume to accept lighter duties in the late 1890s. He still got letters from old convicts who remembered him as a square shooter and looked him up for employment leads on release.

Jim Hume died in May 1904, aged seventy-seven. The great detective often said that no one liked him more than some of the residents of San Quentin and Folsom.

Suggested reading: Richard Dillon, *Wells, Fargo Detective* (Reno: Univ. of Nevada Press, 1986).

DUGOUT OF DEATH

Bat Masterson, a great lawman himself, called Bill Tilghman the greatest in the West. No one really argues. Formerly a buffalo hunter, Tilghman had been an army scout and a deputy sheriff and marshal at Dodge City before he moved to Indian Territory in 1886 to become a deputy U. S. marshal. A handsome man, one hundred eighty pounds of bone and muscle, he received more reward money for capturing outlaws than any other peace officer in the United States for the same period of time.

Probably the greatest moment in the life of this courageous man came on January 7, 1895, when he walked into a room containing eight deadly outlaws, each of whom had him in their sights. How Tilghman escaped that dugout of death provides one of the West's greatest examples of a man with nerves of chilled steel.

Tilghman and Heck Thomas were spearheading the search for Bill Doolin and his Dalton-Doolin gang of outlaws. The work was hard because settlers, sympathetic to the gang, gave warning whenever they saw officers in the area.

On January 6, 1895, Tilghman, with Assistant Deputy Neal Brown and Charlie Bearclaw, rode out of Guthrie to continue the search. They had a covered wagon with equipment and supplies to last a month. Bearclaw drove the team pulling the wagon while the lawmen rode their saddle horses. The weather turned bitter cold.

On the second day out, Bearclaw urged the shivering horses along the dim, snow-blown trail while Tilghman and Brown followed behind, partly sheltered by canvas flapping in the wind. They saw smoke gusting upward from a dugout almost hidden in a dark ravine.

"Let's stop and see if we can get shelter for the night," Tilghman shouted into the storm.

He tied his horse to the rear of the wagon, left his rifle in the wagon, and walked through thick falling snow to the door. He saw no men or horses. No one answered his knock. He pushed the door open and walked in.

An oak fire roared in a wide fireplace at the end of the low-ceilinged room. By its light Tilghman could make out a man sitting in a chair with a Winchester across his knees. The man looked up without speaking. Tilghman recognized him as Bill Dunn, a man who owned a meat market in Pawnee. Dunn had been a lookout for the Dalton-Doolin gang, and helped them dispose of their stolen cattle.

Without showing that he knew who he was talking to, Tilghman walked forward and said, "I was looking for Bill Dunn. He told me once that his fighting dog could whip mine. I was just passing by and thought you might know where he is. I'd like to arrange a match."

Dunn said nothing. As Tilghman moved toward the fire and his eyes adjusted to the low, flickering light, he saw two double bunks on each side of the room. He could not tell if they were occupied, for quilt curtains hung down to cover them. He slowly turned his back to the fire and rubbed his hands to restore circulation. What he saw then tensed every muscle in his body and turned his heart numb.

From each of the eight bunks a rifle muzzle now poked out from the curtain edges to stare him in the face! He stepped to one side, still rubbing his hands. Each rifle muzzle moved to track him.

Tilghman's brain reeled. It would mean instant death to show that he was aware of danger. Without an eyelid twitch or a shake in his voice, he turned to the man in the chair and spoke. "Well, if Bill isn't here, I might as well move on to Pawnee. Need to ford the Cimarron before the storm gets too bad. What's the best way out of here?"

"Same damn way you got in." The man's voice was surly.

"Well, I reckon." Tilghman stamped his feet and rubbed his ears and walked calmly to the door. This time he could hear breathing sounds from the bunks as he walked down the narrow aisle between them. "Well, so long," he flung carelessly over his shoulder as he went out.

Tilghman kept an even pace until he reached the wagon. He wondered every second if bullets would slam into his back. He crawled under the canvas and spoke softly: "Drive ahead, Charlie, and not too fast. Don't look around. Neal, that place is full of outlaws."

They went on to Pawnee, where a large posse started back immediately. They reached the ravine the next morning. Bill Dunn was watching the dugout from a knoll. He rode down to meet the posse.

Dunn explained that he had used a surly tone the day before, as he didn't want the outlaws to think he liked lawmen or recognized Tilghman. He also told Tilghman who the eight men in the bunks were: Bill Doolin, a tall skinny kid who could not read or write; Tulsa Jack Blake, a petty thief who joined the gang so he could prove his worth by gunning a man down; Dynamite Dick Clifton, at forty, the old man — he specialized in blowing safes; Bitter Creek Newcomb, movie-star handsome with a dark mood that foreclosed any questions about his past; Little Dick West — undersized from living out of garbage cans, he grew up without a family; Little Bill Raidler, a Pennsylvania intellectual who quoted Chaucer — he drilled holes in his bullets and filled them with dynamite so they exploded upon entry; Red Buck Weightman, a skilled horse thief; and Charley Pierce, another horse thief who seldom spoke but communicated by his manner of spitting tobacco. Few men in the West could match this emotionally starved group, vengeful and sadistic, in their hate for lawmen.

Dunn also explained how Tilghman had saved his own life by his demonstration of cold nerve. In the end, however, even more had been required. When the outlaws saw Tilghman approaching, they knew they could not get out of the dugout without meeting him face to face. They all knew who he was, and they had no desire for that confrontation. So they had hurriedly hung up the blanket curtains and hid. They would have shot upon seeing any sign of discovery. But they saw nothing, not the slightest sign of fear.

Even then, as soon as Tilghman had closed the door behind him, Red Buck jumped out of his bunk to shoot the marshal. Bill Doolin restrained him, saying, "Bill Tilghman's too good a man to shoot in the back. If you kill him, there'll be a hundred here by morning and they'll dynamite this place off the earth."

Tilghman never forgot that Doolin may have saved his life. When he arrested the man at Eureka Springs, Arkansas, in January, 1896, he risked his own life to take Doolin alive. It would have been easy to kill him in the struggle.

So one of the best lawmen in the West survived on raw nerve and the respect he had earned from outlaws to fight some more days. In 1924, when he was seventy and again a marshal in a rowdy Oklahoma town, Bill Tilghman was fatally shot in the back by a drunken prohibition officer.

Suggested reading: Glenn Shirley, *Six-gun and Silver Star* (Albuquerque: Univ. of New Mexico Press, 1955).

ARIZONA RANGER CAPTAIN

Burt Mossman was first, last, and most of the time a cattleman, but he had a short, spectacular career as a peace officer.

Mossman was thirty years old when he stepped off the train in Holbrook, Arizona, in January, 1898. A cowboy met him with a saddle horse for his ride to the million acre Hash Knife ranch, which Mossman was taking over as superintendent. Mossman knew the outfit had been losing a thousand calves a year from their fifty thousand cow herd, and had never shown a profit.

His cowboy escort told Mossman that he knew where rustlers were butchering some of the ranch's calves.

"Let's go there," Mossman said. "I'll go to headquarters later."

He followed the cowboy, captured the rustlers, and brought them and the incriminating evidence back to town.

The sheriff, impressed, made Mossman a deputy on the spot. Mossman spent most of his time chasing rustlers and horse thieves, leaving the operation of the ranch to the foreman. For the first time in its fifteen-year history the ranch turned a profit.

But Arizona was full of train and stage robbers, and murderers from other territories and Mexico. Something had to be done. The governor persuaded Mossman to organize a company of rangers and to become its captain. Mossman agreed on condition that he could hire his own men, take orders from nobody, and name his successor. Even then he would only do it for a year; he didn't think he would live any longer.

News of the new company of lawmen convinced some bandits to seek other pastures, even though they had killed six lawmen in the preceding six months. One who didn't leave was Augustin Chacon, a Mexican citizen. Chacon had killed at least thirty Americans. Lawmen had been unable to bring him to justice.

Once while Chacon was awaiting execution, his girlfriend had slipped hacksaw blades into him, wrapped in a prayer book. Then she flirted with the jailer until he took her into the ·Sheriff's office to make love. As other Mexican prisoners played the guitar and concertina to hide the sawing noise, Chacon escaped. Two days later he was to have been hanged on the gallows, just outside his cell.·

Capturing such a cunning and elusive bandit was a challenge. At some risk to his own life Mossman rode into Mexican mountains where two criminals were hiding out. One of them, Burt Alvord, a friend of Chacon, was wanted for train robbing and cattle rustling. Alvord, a one-time deputy sheriff and marshal who had turned to crime, had been recently shot, and Mossman knew he could not get medical attention while on the dodge. The other outlaw, Billy Stiles, was a train robber who knew both Chacon and Alvord. Mossman wanted him to act as his messenger to contact Alvord.

He found both men, told them they could earn light sentences for cooperation, and Alvord could get the medical attention he needed. The men agreed to take Burt to Chacon's hideout in Mexico, introducing him as a horse thief.

The pressure of bringing this brave lawman into the hideout of the most vicious criminal in North America was too much for Alvord. He rode away from their camp, first warning Mossman that Stiles was planning a double cross.

Mossman foiled the double cross and single-handedly captured both Chacon and Stiles. Of course it was an illegal kidnapping of a Mexican citizen, but desperate needs led to desperate actions. Burt Mossman had ended one of the most demanding manhunts in the history of the Old West, and Chacon's criminal life was over; he was soon hanged.

Mossman turned Stiles loose after they reached the United States. Stiles left the territory, spent some time in China and was eventually killed in Nevada. Alvord surrendered and got the light sentence promised by Mossman.

Mossman had tamed an empire of lawlessness with thirteen rangers. He lost one ranger killed; others were wounded. Mossman resigned and returned to ranching, this time in Dakota territory. He had been born on an Illinois farm, the oldest of nine children. His father was a major in the Union Army during the Civil War. Mossman's son, a major in the United States Army Air Corps, was shot down and killed in World War Two.

Suggested reading: Carl W. Breihan, *Great Lawmen of the West* (New York: Bonanza Books, 1963).

NOT YOUR TYPICAL MARSHAL

Mike Meagher was not a typical trail town marshal. He had only killed one man when he, himself, was gunned down in Caldwell, Kansas, in December 1881.

A cheerful Irishman, Mike started out as marshal in Wichita. After three years relying on cool nerve to handle killers, thieves, and prostitutes, Mike took a year off to serve as deputy United States marshal. During that year he also scouted against Indians as a first lieutenant in the Kansas militia.

But Mike missed being a city marshal. In 1875 he won his old office back and also got married. Twenty-four-year-old Jenny was from Ohio, and she and thirty-two-year-old Mike looked forward to their life together. She would keep the home while Mike made his mark as a community leader.

Re-elected in 1876, Mike still avoided firing his pistol until New Year's Day, 1877. On that day, Sylvester Powell, normally a quiet stage driver, got drunk and for some reason grabbed E. R. Dennison's horse. Dennison smiled as he protested, but Powell, mean-mad, swung a heavy neck yoke into Dennison, permanently crippling him. Mike arrested Powell on Dennison's complaint.

When Powell's employer paid the fine that evening and obtained the prisoner's release, Powell threatened to kill Mike. As he walked out of the jail he snarled, "I'll put daylight through you the next time I see you."

Later that evening Powell started looking for Mike, bragging that his foe had spent his last day on earth. Powell found Mike at the public toilet behind a saloon. He began shooting immediately. The light was poor, and he hit Mike in the leg and hand. Powell ran into an alley, and Mike ran around the block to the main street and waited. As Powell ran out of the alley, into view, Mike fired once. Powell fell dead, a bullet in his heart.

Mike and Jenny moved to Caldwell, and he went into the saloon business. But Mike still heard the public calling for leadership, and he became mayor in 1880. He was soon caught up in the tension between merchants like himself who wanted law and order and those who wanted a wide open trail town that Texas cowboys would enjoy. In that atmosphere Mike, along with the city marshal and the complete city police force, were arrested by the county sheriff for complicity in the shooting of a former marshal.

They were all freed after evidence in court showed their innocence. Mike was also arrested and fined for running an illegal gambling game.

The tension came to a head for Mike on December 17, 1881. Mike had not sought re-election as mayor, but was now working as a carpenter. Jim Talbot had come up the Chisholm Trail with a trail herd from Texas several months before. A born trouble maker, Talbot stayed in Caldwell and frequently threatened to kill people, including Mike. There was a rumor that he was a cousin of Sylvester Powell, the man Mike had killed before.

In December 1881, Talbot's threats were directed to one of the editors of a Caldwell newspaper. Early one Saturday morning, Talbot and about five friends were drinking and in an ugly mood. Mike went to the home of Marshal John Wilson, asking him to come down town and prevent a riot.

Wilson arrested one of the men, Tom Love, and disarmed him. The rest of the gang threatened to rescue Love, and Wilson asked Mike to help him. The gang attacked and got Love away. As they dispersed, one of them said, "Meagher is the man we want, and Meagher is the man we'll have."

Shortly after noon, Marshal Wilson arrested another of the men, Jim Martin, for shooting his revolver. Then Talbot, Love, and a third man re-captured Martin. Again, Mike was helping the marshal.

In the gunfight that followed, Mike was shot in the chest. Asked if he was hurt, Mike replied, "Yes, tell Jenny that I have got it at last."

Mike was carried into a barber shop. He died in about thirty minutes.

Suggested reading: Nyle Miller & Joseph Snell, *Great Gunfighters of the Kansas Cowtowns, 1867-1868* (Lincoln: Univ. of Nebraska Press, 1967).

THREE-STATE PURSUIT

Brown's Park, the mountainous country south of the common corner of Utah, Wyoming and Colorado, sheltered outlaws from the earliest days of the Old West. On February 28, 1898, Sheriff Charles W. Neiman of Routt County, Colorado, rode west from Steamboat Springs toward the park with warrants for John Bennett and Patrick Johnson. The warrants, signed by Justice of the Peace J. S. Hoy, charged cattle theft. Neiman picked up deputy Ethan Allen Farnham in Craig, and they rode on to Boyd Vaughn's ranch.

Vaughn joined the officers, as he had lost some horses the previous fall, and he suspected they were in the park. As they approached Vermillion Creek, hoping to reach the Bassett ranch by nightfall, the men saw three riders ahead, leading a packhorse. Neiman tried to catch up with the riders to ask if they had seen anything of Bennett and Johnson. When the riders speeded up to stay ahead, Neiman suspected the party included the men he sought.

Neiman was partly right, but the group ahead was far more dangerous than he thought. It included Johnson, who was not only a cattle thief, but had just murdered fifteen-year-old Willie Strang in Wyoming. As Johnson and Bennett were fleeing from Wyoming, they had run into Harry Tracy and David Lant, who had escaped from the Utah state prison and were hiding out in Brown's Park, waiting to join Butch Cassidy's gang. Bennett, with only cattle stealing charges on his head, had ridden off by himself. The other three were the men Neiman had seen and tried to catch.

The officers and Vaughn did reach the Bassett ranch that night, where they learned from Willie Strang's older brother, who worked there, about his brother's murder, and that Deputy Sheriff Pete Swanson of Sweetwater County, Wyoming, was leading a posse searching for Johnson. Not trusting Bassett, whom Neiman suspected gave information to outlaws on the dodge, the sheriff got the Strang boy aside and told him that he thought he knew where his brother's killer was. Strang rode out that night to gather a posse and see if word could be sent to the Wyoming deputy.

Shortly after midnight a five man posse rode in. The five new men joined Neiman, his deputy, and Vaughn when they rode out before daylight. They soon picked up the outlaws' trail, and by mid afternoon they found a small campfire which had been hurriedly abandoned, leaving horses, equipment, and supplies behind.

Sheriff Neiman was one of the outstanding law officers of the Old West. He had imagination, common sense, and good judgment. He looked up at caves and rock outcroppings and knew the fugitives already had the posse in their sights. The posse could not attack without losing men. Without food or bedding, and with winter temperatures dropping low at night, the outlaws would probably be glad to surrender the next day. Even then, it took some argument for Neiman to persuade the posse to return to the Bassett ranch for the night.

The next morning the posse picked up the outlaw's trail in the snow and followed it until they knew they were close to their prey. Again, the sheriff wanted to play a waiting game, but the volunteer posse insisted on getting it over with. Neiman finally gave in. He posted Vaughn and Ebb Bassett to watch the flat country, in case the outlaws tried to double back and escape, and another man to watch the horses. Then he led the others up a steep slope.

A shot rang out, and Valentine Hoy fell dead in his tracks. The outlaws had every advantage. After a two hour standoff, Neiman persuaded the posse to retreat, again returning to the Bassett ranch.

In the meantime, Bassett and Vaughn had seen Bennett riding a horse in the distance. Bennett knew Bassett but did not know Vaughn. The two men rode up to the fugitive, and Bassett invited him to spend the night at the ranch. Vaughn, posing as a rancher looking for horses, kept riding. As soon as he was out of sight, he put his horse into a gallop and caught up with Neiman.

Before becoming sheriff, Neiman had been foreman of a large ranch in the area, and he knew all the back trails. He reached the Bassett Ranch before Ebb Bassett and Bennett got there. The surprised outlaw was easily captured when he rode up.

Learning from Bennett that two of the outlaws were escapees from the Utah prison, Neiman sent Bill Pidgeon on a ninety mile ride to Vernal for William Preece, sheriff of Uintah County, Utah. That night, the Bassett Ranch bunkhouse served as Bennett's jail.

The next morning, Neiman left Deputy Farnham to guard the prisoner while he again led the posse out after the three outlaws. At noon seven masked men, with guns drawn, surrounded Farnham, seized prisoner Bennett, and hanged him from the corral gate. When Neiman returned that evening to the Bassett Ranch, still without the outlaws, he was dismayed to learn of the lynching.

Knowing that the outlaws could not leave Brown's Park without going past one of three sheep camps, the next morning Neiman split the posse into three parts, sending one to each camp.

The group headed by Deputy Farnham and the Wyoming deputy captured the outlaws as they approached one of the sheep camps. Riding back to the Bassett Ranch, they met J. S. Hoy, who was on his way to pick up the remains of his brother. J. S. Hoy was the justice of the peace for the area, and he agreed to hold the magistrate's examination the next day.

"Which one of you killed my brother?" Hoy asked.

"Well, it was sure one of us," Tracy said contemptuously.

The examination was held in the living room of the Bassett ranchhouse. The prisoners looked hardly human, their clothing in shreds and their swollen feet wrapped in rags. The audience of hollow-eyed, grim men, most of whom had had little sleep during the long chase, wanted to dispense the same kind of justice that had been given to Bennett, who, of course, had had nothing to do with killing Hoy or the Strang boy. But J. S. Hoy was an educated, cultured man. In spite of the intense feelings about his brother's death, his examination was fair and perfectly legal.

That night over sixty men — members of the three state posses and other local residents — were at the Bassett ranch, and there was much talk about lynching. Sheriff Neiman kept up a night-long vigil, going from group to group to discourage the talk.

The next day Neiman delivered Johnson to the Wyoming deputy. Still fearful of a lynching, he and Deputy Farnham took the other two prisoners, Tracy and Lant, by back country cattle trails to the jail at Hahn's Peak in Routt County. It was not a very good jail, and shortly after their arrival the men beat Neiman unconscious and escaped. When Neiman recovered he traveled to Steamboat Springs and boarded the stage, convinced that the escaped prisoners would try to take the stage out of the area.

When the stage was eight miles out of Steamboat Springs, Tracy and Lant tried to board it. They opened the door to see Neiman's pistol in their faces.

"Welcome, Tracy," Neiman said. "Step right in, your breakfast is waiting."

Tracy took the men to the Aspen jail, a much better one. Although Neiman had warned the jailer in Aspen that the men were dangerous, Tracy was able to carve a gun out of soap and the prisoners escaped again.

David Lant had had enough. A Utah farm boy who had gone to prison for burglary, he split from Tracy, joined the army, and served with distinction in the Philippines during the Spanish-American War. Apparently he was never prosecuted for his prison and jail escapes.

Tracy was just at the beginning of his life of crime. He and another prisoner escaped from the Oregon state prison in June, 1902, killing three men to get away. A few days later Tracy feared that his fellow escapee, who was also his brother-in-law, was weakening. Tracy shot him in the back of the head.

For two months, Tracy avoided hundreds of pursuers, some with bloodhounds, in Oregon and Washington. On one of his crimes before this, Tracy had captured a passenger train. Now he exceeded that feat by confiscating a gasoline launch with its four-man crew on Puget Sound. He made the crew cruise the sound all day for his benefit. As they sailed by the federal prison at McNeil Island, Tracy wanted to show his marksmanship by shooting guards on the walls. Fortunately the ship's captain talked him out of that.

Tracy shot it out with a posse after leaving the launch, killing three more men. Sometimes he would call a sheriff on the telephone to tell him that he was still in the area. Finally, on August 5, Tracy, surrounded by another posse and lying wounded in a barley field, shot himself to death. America's greatest manhunt was over.

In a macabre footnote to the Brown's Park pursuit, William Pidgeon, the posse member who had made the fast ride to summon the Utah sheriff, was killed later that year by one Ike Lee in a canyon in Brown's Park. Pidgeon had originally come into the country with Jack Bennett, the small time rustler who got hanged by the vigilantes. Eventually Lee gave himself up in Vernal, Utah. But the night after Lee killed Pidgeon, a local rancher, Charley Teters, rode by Lee's camp and stopped to talk. Teters noticed that Lee and his friends were cooking something in a large kettle.

"What are you guys cooking?" Teters asked.

"Soup," Lee replied. "You want to have a look?"

Teters looked in the boiling pot and saw Pidgeon's head, the meat already separating from the bones. He learned that someone in Lee's group knew a doctor who wanted a human skull. The group was getting Pidgeon's head ready for market.

Suggested reading: John R. Burroughs, *Where the Old West Stayed Young* (New York: Wm. Morrow and Co., 1962).

ORDERING INFORMATION

True Tales of the Old West is projected for 36 volumes.

Proposed titles include:

Warriors and Chiefs	In print
Soldiers	In print
Native Women	In print
Mountain Men	In print
Pioneer Women	In print
Ranchers and Cowboys	In print
Horses and Riders	In print
Miners	In print
Entertainers	In print
Dogs and Masters	In print
Outlaws	In print
Frontiersmen	In print
Gamblers	In print
Lawmen	In print
Scouts	In print
Homesteaders	Soon to appear
Vigilantes	Soon to appear
Writers	Soon to appear
Explorers	Under way
Courts & Lawyers	Under way
Railroaders	Under way
Merchants	Started
Army Women	Started
Children	Started
Duelists	Started

Ask at your bookstore or write:

PIONEER PRESS
Box 216
Carson City, NV 89702-0216
(775) 888-9867